NEW DIRECTIONS FOR HIGHER EDUCATION

Martin Kramer
EDITOR-IN-CHIEF

An Administrator's Guide for Responding to Campus Crime: From Prevention to Liability

Richard Fossey
Louisiana State University

Michael Clay Smith
University of Southern Mississippi

EDITORS

Number 95, Fall 1996

JOSSEY-BASS PUBLISHERS
San Francisco

AN ADMINISTRATOR'S GUIDE FOR RESPONDING TO CAMPUS CRIME: FROM
PREVENTION TO LIABILITY
Richard Fossey, Michael Clay Smith (eds.)
New Directions for Higher Education, no. 95
Volume XXIV, Number 3
Martin Kramer, Editor-in-Chief

Microfilm copies of issues and articles are available in 16mm and 35mm,
as well as microfiche in 105mm, through University Microfilms Inc., 300
North Zeeb Road, Ann Arbor, Michigan 48106-1346.

ISSN 0271-0560   ISBN 0-7879-9873-7

NEW DIRECTIONS FOR HIGHER EDUCATION is part of The Jossey-Bass
Higher and Adult Education Series and is published quarterly by Jossey-
Bass Inc., Publishers, 350 Sansome Street, San Francisco, California
94104-1342. Periodicals postage paid at San Francisco, California, and at
additional mailing offices. POSTMASTER: Send address changes to New
Directions for Higher Education, Jossey-Bass Inc., Publishers, 350 Sansome Street, San Francisco, California 94104-1342.

SUBSCRIPTIONS cost $52.00 for individuals and $79.00 for institutions,
agencies, and libraries.

EDITORIAL CORRESPONDENCE should be sent to the Editor-in-Chief, Martin
Kramer, 2807 Shasta Road, Berkeley, California 94708-2011.

Cover photograph and random dot by Richard Blair/Color & Light © 1990.

TCF   Manufactured in the United States of America on Lyons Falls
       Pathfinder Tradebook. This paper is acid-free and 100 percent
totally chlorine-free.

CONTENTS

EDITORS' NOTES

As a general rule, college campuses are safer from crime than their surrounding cities and towns. Made up of faculty, students, and a supportive staff, colleges and universities are communities of learning with relatively few criminals. And, removed as they usually are from poverty, overcrowding, and the desperate socioeconomic conditions that breed crime, colleges are often oases of calm and order in an increasingly dangerous world.

Nevertheless, in spite of their relative safety, colleges and universities have a growing concern about campus crime. Law enforcement budgets have increased, high-profile crime prevention programs have been put in place, and, in general, college administrators have devoted an increasing amount of time to campus safety and security. Why has this been so?

We can think of three reasons. First, courts are increasingly willing to hold colleges and universities liable for damages when students or staff are injured by a crime that might have been prevented had proper precautions been taken. To prevent lawsuits, many higher education institutions are highlighting crime prevention in their routine risk management programs.

Second, college students and their families are becoming more sophisticated consumers and are demanding better protection against campus crime. As the cost of a college education goes up, students and their families are looking closer at the quality of services being provided, and these services include law enforcement and campus security. Media attention on campus crime has probably contributed to this phenomenon, providing students with a great deal of information about the crimes that take place on the nation's college campuses.

Third, over the past ten years, federal legislation has been passed specifically addressed to preventing campus crime. The Ramstad Amendment and the Student Right-to-Know and Campus Security Act, in particular, have increased the responsibility of higher education institutions for preventing crime and providing services to crime victims.

All three of these developments have contributed to a growing need for campus administrators to learn more about campus crime and to become more skilled in preventing it. This volume was written to address that need.

The volume begins with three overview chapters. In Chapter One, Carole B. Dahlem provides guidance in developing an overall crime prevention program. In Chapter Two, Margaret D. Smith discusses the civil liability issues that often accompany campus crime. In Chapter Three, Donald D. Gehring outlines the growing responsibility of campus administrators to comply with and enforce federal laws and regulations that relate to campus crime.

The last four chapters deal with specific campus crime problems. In Chapter Four, we outline the liability and prevention issues surrounding campus rape. In Chapter Five, Steven D. Gordon discusses college and university liability for fraud, waste, and abuse in federally funded grants and projects. In

Chapter Six, Jerome W. D. Stokes and Allen W. Groves explore legal issues that arise when an offer of admission is withdrawn after an applicant's prior criminal record is discovered. Finally, in Chapter Seven, we review several discrete crime issues, including training programs for campus police officers and the application of copyright law to college course materials.

Although each of the contributing authors brings a particular perspective and type of expertise to the volume, all of the chapters are written from a practical perspective. The editors hope that this volume will be a useful handbook for college administrators; one they can refer to again and again as they engage in the task of making their campuses safe from crime.

Richard Fossey
Michael Clay Smith
Editors

RICHARD FOSSEY is associate professor of education law and policy, Louisiana State University.

MICHAEL CLAY SMITH is professor of criminal justice, University of Southern Mississippi.

Everyone on campus has a role in reducing the risks of crime.

First Things First: Developing a Crime Prevention Program

Carole B. Dahlem

Gone are the days when security budgets and safety concerns were low priority items for college and university administrators, parents, and students. Crimes on campus are no longer viewed by the public and the media as minor mischief and the exceptional collegiate experience. For parents and incoming students, crime is perceived as a problem of life-threatening proportions. Crime statistics and campus security resources are now factors that receive prime consideration by many who are choosing a college.

Is campus crime a real problem, or only a perceived one? Actual crime risks vary substantially from campus to campus. A 1990 *USA Today* survey showed that the rate for all types of campus crimes was only about half the overall national crime rate of 57 per 1,000 people ("Violent Crime No Stranger on Campuses," 1990), yet some campuses have experienced very high rates of crime. In today's educational marketplace, where institutions contend against one another for students, faculty, and financial support, the mere perception of crime risk is as important as the reality.

Campus crime is, of course, a reflection of the rampant crime that plagues and subdues much of contemporary American life. According to federal figures, nearly eleven million Americans experience violent crimes each year (Bureau of Justice Statistics, 1995), and Americans are more likely to be victims of violent crime than to die from cancer, injury, or in a fire (Bureau of Justice Statistics, 1988). The strange thing is that people seem to spend more time studying the health benefits of food and exercise than they do learning strategies to avoid becoming victims of crime; the latter is certainly a significant health risk.

Obviously a campus administrator would prefer to prevent crime before it happens rather than to deal with a crisis situation. In addressing the issue of

NEW DIRECTIONS FOR HIGHER EDUCATION, no. 95, Fall 1996 © Jossey-Bass Publishers campus crime, an administrator should consider a prevention program at the outset, not as an afterthought. This chapter will briefly show how crime prevention theories have developed with an eye toward the practical application of these theories today.

From Burlesque to Crime Prevention

Modern crime prevention methods have an unlikely source: Henry Fielding, the English novelist and playwright who is best known today for his risqué novel *The Amorous Adventures of Tom Jones*. In the mid 1700s, Fielding was a criminal court judge in London. As the victims and perpetrators of the city's crimes paraded through his court, he became concerned that the old system was not sufficient for the task. Police forces as we know them did not exist, and the legal system could act only to punish—albeit very severely—the few offenders who were caught. Fielding theorized that a police force could be effective in eliminating existing crime. He also believed it important to take steps to prevent crime in the future. To meet this second goal, he recommended an active organization of citizen householders as well as social initiatives to remove some of the causes of crime and the conditions in which crime flourished.

Fielding was the first person to actively collect and collate crime incident reports to discover crime patterns. He sent out proclamations encouraging citizens who had suffered crimes to "bring or send the best description they can of such robberies etc. with the time and place and circumstances of the event to Henry Fielding, Esquire at his home in Bow Street." This is an activity we recognize today as crime analysis, an important aspect of crime prevention.

A century later another important figure in British history, Sir Robert Peel, played a role in the advancement of crime prevention as part of his formulation of the Metropolitan Police Force. (The force is still known as the "Bobbies," after Sir Robert's nickname Bobby.) As Prime Minister, he signed the Peelian Reform Act of 1829 into law. Its police reforms are considered the foundations of modern law enforcement. The new force was to be government controlled (instead of privately employed) and was to be organized along military lines. Officers would be trained and would wear uniforms. Peel also insisted that the distribution of crime information was essential for effective police action.

Peel's standing field instructions for the Metropolitan Police Force reflect the attitude of wise campus administrators today: "It should be understood at the outset that the principal objective to be achieved in policing is the prevention of crime. . . . All the other objectives of a police establishment will thus be better affected by prevention rather than by the detection, apprehension, and punishment of the offender after he has succeeded in committing the crime."

It was not until 1950 that a law enforcement agency gave the public a role to play in crime prevention. A British police department, overwhelmed by high burglary rates, put together a traveling display that featured a three-minute film showing home owners security treatments and habits that would ward off bur-glars. The drop in burglary rates was so impressive that the British dedicated an entire law enforcement division in the Home Office to crime prevention (National Crime Prevention Institute, 1986, pp. 12–14).

The concept of crime prevention was introduced to American law enforce-ment by John C. Klotter, who studied the British model of burglary prevention on a Ford Foundation grant. In 1971 he established the National Crime Pre-vention Institute within the School of Police Administration at the University of Louisville (National Crime Prevention Institute, 1986, pp. 2–6). The focus of the institute was on crimes against property and crimes by strangers. It stressed crime analysis, community program development, and security hard-ware. The issue of crime between acquaintances would have to wait to be addressed in the future.

Even with this history, scientific crime prevention is all too often ignored. Two factors account for this. First, police priorities have, not surprisingly, tended to favor the more glamorous tasks of detection and apprehension of criminals. Second, in a world of limited resources and increasing demands for police services, most police agencies are constantly playing catch-up and have little opportunity to be proactive. This is where prioritizing is a must.

Judging Security Proposals

A classic definition of crime prevention is the anticipation, recognition, and appraisal of a crime risk and the initiation of some action to remove or reduce the risk. To be successful, a crime prevention program should develop ongo-ing collaboration among all sectors of the campus community: students, fac-ulty, security forces, student services personnel, and maintenance employees. In addition, those in charge of crime prevention should be knowledgeable about the broad spectrum of crime prevention measures and skilled in choos-ing the most effective measures for a particular campus environment.

Unless campus security personnel have crime prevention expertise, they are likely to squander scarce security dollars developing ineffective security measures. Indeed, two primary areas in which campus administrators often fail in their attempts to provide adequate security for students and prevent crime are in basing a response on inaccurately perceived problems and crime myths and being unable to judge the effectiveness of existing and proposed security efforts.

Criteria for Judging Security Proposals

There are three general approaches used by crime prevention specialists to address a security threat: informational, mechanical, and human. While all can be directed to a particular security problem, they are often introduced to a spe-cific environment one at a time, based on evaluations of effectiveness and cost (Crowe, 1991).

Informational Applications. Informational security applications are usually the most effective and least costly of the three crime prevention approaches. The informational application is based on the concept of furnishing the community needed information about crime prevention and giving community members a role in protecting themselves and their property. Sometimes no further security application is needed.

Crime analysis is the foundation for other informational applications: crime alerts, prevention programming, and neighborhood watch activities. These are carried out through various forms of communication such as pamphlets, training programs, media relations, and statistics preparation. Informational applications also include the development of specific campus operating procedures, including key control, accurate job descriptions, employee background checks, signage, and policy enforcement. Good information increases officers' ability to direct the right response to the right problem, giving them more than hunches or personal opinions as to the nature, time, and place to expect crime before they are deployed into the streets.

An informational approach to a rash of thefts in a campus administrative building might involve the following steps: first, residents could be alerted to the time of day that thefts are occurring from unlocked offices. This could be accomplished through posting of notices, with updates. Next, a security presentation could be made to discuss the securing of property, suggest ways to make the workplace safer, and introduce building security policies and methods for responding to suspicious behavior.

Another aspect of an informational application is the use of crime prevention design concepts in the campus design process. The concept known as Crime Prevention Through Environmental Design (CPTED) employs natural surveillance and access (meaning the use of occupants of a building to oversee entrances, common areas, and so on) as well as landscaping, lighting, and signage to create boundaries and differentiate private space from public space.

Natural surveillance in the design process would include such things as use of glass in doors or the addition of windows in administrative office areas to help monitor the building entrance and hallways. Together with strategic placement of office desks, personnel then have the ability to help monitor their work space during office hours. The effect on users is welcoming; for those who are looking for a criminal opportunity it is uncomfortable and unwelcome surveillance.

There is generally no cost to informational applications, yet they are effective because they involve the active participation of people. Informed residents become security resources and extensions of a systemwide crime prevention effort. However, to be effective, informational approaches require collaboration, monitoring, and a long-term commitment from senior decision makers.

Mechanical Applications. Mechanical applications are the second most effective and second most costly security applications. Mechanical applications involve security hardware and constructed barriers. Examples include door locks, alarm systems, burglar bars, emergency phones, video cameras, card access systems, walls, fences, gates, electronic door access systems, scream alarms, chemical sprays, personal alarms, and weapons.

Mechanical applications can be very expensive initially, and they are often expensive to maintain. They sometimes require a human to monitor the equipment (as in video surveillance and alarm monitoring), which adds an ongoing cost to the initial installation cost. These applications often appear to be effective; it is true that they demand less involvement from the people who live or work in the area. An apartment resident can "buzz" a visitor into a building without having to walk to the entrance door. However, mechanical security devices sometimes can be circumvented or deactivated by those intent on criminal mischief.

For these reasons, security hardware can sometimes create an illusion of safety that is not warranted. A video camera in a parking garage does not mean that someone will actually see that someone needs help; it may simply record the attack. Car alarms lose effectiveness when people become so accustomed to them that they pay no attention.

Finally, security personnel must remember that information is often important to successful mechanical applications. Locks only provide building security if occupants use them; alarms are effective only if they are activated. Using an entire building project's security budget to install high-impact plastic on first-floor windows is not a good idea when most forced entries are through doors.

Human Applications. Human applications are often the least effective and most costly of the three approaches to crime prevention. Examples of human applications are door guards, police patrols, and attendants for surveillance of video monitors, parking lots, and security or information desks. On the other hand, one of the benefits of the human application is the deterrence often afforded by a responsible or uniformed presence. In addition, the presence of security personnel often makes people feel safer.

This human application is costly because of the reoccurring expenses for salary, benefits, and uniforms. It costs approximately $60,000 in the first year to hire, train, and equip one new police officer. The expense of recommending a human application can be reduced by using nonprofessional personnel for some functions, such as the monitoring of video camera systems, or by changing a door guard position to an information and receptionist function.

Another disadvantage of the human application is that residents or occupants may rely on an officer alone to be responsible for building security, and thus fail to take part of the responsibility themselves. The residents may no longer feel they should check doors or question the presence of a stranger. And, unlike the other two applications, the effect of deterrence is apparent only when the human is within view.

Unlike other security approaches, the human application cannot stand alone. To be effective, it must be used in conjunction with informational and mechanical applications. Because of its expense and limitations, the human security application should be the last application applied to a security risk or concern.

Colleges Lead the Way

Recently, crime prevention innovations have been coming from college crime prevention programs. Many of these innovations have been stimulated by the array of recent legislation and court decisions that have created standards of university accountability that now exceed those applicable to other public institutions. (See Chapter Two on liability issues and Chapter Three on legislation and regulations.) Unlike off-campus governing authorities (even in primary and secondary schools), institutions of higher education are required by law to regularly disseminate crime information, to post special crime alerts, to offer crime prevention programming, and to develop policies and support services to address specific crime risks (especially sexual assault). This legal environment, together with increased public awareness of campus crime risks, has pushed colleges and universities to become an important part of the national effort to find solutions to crime.

The unique environment of the campus lends itself to new approaches, including the following:

Communication with the community. Timely alerts to students and employees of crime danger on campus are mandated by law. In addition to bulletin boards and flyers, some campuses have employed newer methods of communication to warn of crime danger, including the Internet, fax, e-mail, electronic bulletin boards, the World Wide Web, and voice mail.

Education and mediation. Many campus crime prevention programs stress education, information, and collaboration rather than security hardware and patrolling officers. Violence between acquaintances is recognized as a crime, and programs that advocate conflict resolution and mediation are viewed as new crime prevention applications.

Campus design. Acknowledging the relationship between the physical design of buildings and grounds and the occurrence of crimes is a natural evolution of the campus planning process. The CPTED concept can be brought to bear at the beginning of the design process rather than trying to retrofit a building after it is completed. A growing body of information now exists to assist planners in designing a building or outdoor space so that it is more attractive and safer for friendly users and less supportive of criminal activity.

Information and support systems. Various campus departments can designate a crime prevention specialist who can provide information to help prevent crime and support for victims after a crime occurs. Such specialists can link victims to a network of resources, including counseling, medical, and law enforcement personnel, thereby helping students and employees to continue their studies and careers despite the trauma of crime.

Campus policing. Police response time is often much faster on campus than in the surrounding community. Municipal and county police response time can be quite slow because of personnel shortages and the distances that police must travel to get to crime scenes. A recent study found that nationwide only 44 percent of victimizations were responded to by police within ten minutes, and 11 percent were not responded to within one hour (Bureau of Justice Statistics, 1994).

An Emerging Concern: Off-Campus Crime Rates

Even if the campus itself enjoys a low crime rate, crime in surrounding neighborhoods may have to be addressed. If outside crime spills over into the campus, either the campus must insulate itself with prophylactic devices such as walls, fences, gates, and surveillance hardware and personnel, or steps must be taken to ameliorate crime risks within off-campus neighborhoods, or both. If students and employees are at risk as they venture beyond the campus boundaries, safety on the institution's own property may become immaterial. This is particularly true if the institution relies heavily on off-campus student housing. Often students on a budget and without cars are forced to live in areas high in crime and in housing that has poor security hardware and little police protection.

Colleges and universities, in many cases, have been slow to help neighborhood groups and area businesses address the life-quality issues associated with being situated near a campus. Zoning violations, noise, parking problems, trash, and crime commonly are associated with dense populations of short-term renters (which, after all, is precisely what students are). Likewise, many students are unused to living independently in a neighborhood. These factors have led homeowners and city administrators to label the areas as student ghettos and to ignore problems there.

Programs and services that teach students to find safe housing and live as good neighbors can be seen as part of an institution's educational mission. It is also in the long-term interest of colleges and universities to join neighborhood groups and encourage the enforcement of laws and codes that hold students and rental property owners accountable for quality-of-life issues, including crime risks.

Conclusion: The Role of the Crime Prevention Specialist

Every campus should have a crime prevention specialist, and larger institutions should have a staff devoted to prevention and victim support. If there are ten officers on a campus force, at least two of them should be full-time crime prevention specialists.

Those selected for crime prevention work should view it as a long-term training commitment, and they should, at least eventually, have sufficient rank within the campus police force to have a significant impact upon the force's decision-making processes. These officers should have a broad base of interests and have the ability to solve problems and collaborate with others on security issues within the entire university community.

The training menu for crime prevention specialists should include crime analysis, program development and implementation, training methods, security hardware applications, media relations, and CPTED techniques. The officers also should be trained in lighting, landscaping, and urban design concepts and should be familiar with building terminology.

Through the use of research and crime analysis, trained crime prevention practitioners can direct scarce resources to the right targets, furnish the right information, and recommend the appropriate security applications for the future. They can help to mobilize the efforts of the entire campus community to create and maintain a campus that looks like, feels like, and is a safe learning and working environment.

References

Bureau of Justice Statistics. *Report to the Nation on Crime and Justice.* (2nd ed.) Washington, D.C.: U.S. Department of Justice, 1988.

Bureau of Justice Statistics. *Violent Crime: National Crime Victimization Survey.* Washington, D.C.: U.S. Department of Justice, 1994.

Bureau of Justice Statistics. *Criminal Victimization 1993.* Washington, D.C.: U.S. Department of Justice, 1995.

Crowe, T. D. *Crime Prevention Through Environmental Design.* Boston: Butterworth-Heinemann, 1991.

National Crime Prevention Institute. *Understanding Crime Prevention.* Boston: Butterworth-Heinemann, 1986.

"Violent Crime No Stranger on Campuses." *USA Today,* Nov. 29, 1990, p. 1.

CAROLE B. DAHLEM *is director of Tulane University's Office of Crime Prevention and Victim Resources and is a national consultant on crime prevention applications.*

Courts hold that colleges have duties to warn, to protect, and to keep promises of security.

Crime Liability Suits and Campus Administrators

Margaret D. Smith

Campus crime has become both a marketing issue and an asset preservation factor for America's colleges and universities. Those who govern and manage the nation's campuses must endeavor to lessen crime risks—and the perception of them—in order to protect institutional image, enhance student recruitment, and avoid costly lawsuits stemming from an alleged failure to protect students and employees from criminal miscreants.

Admittedly, amelioration of crime problems and skillful adaptation of risk management techniques are relatively new concerns for academic administrators; the ravages of campus crime, and the high visibility given the topic in the news media, emerged as major issues in the late 1980s, and promise to so remain in the foreseeable future. A few decades ago it was unthinkable for a student to sue a college or university about anything, yet today it has become commonplace. In lawsuits brought by crime victims, not just institutional assets and reputations are in jeopardy; now individual administrators and employees are sometimes sued personally, with the prospect that they could have to pay to defend the suit and any resulting award of damages out of their own pockets.

How best to meet the challenge? The first step for college and university administrators is to understand the legal theories, or grounds, for suits that have been successfully asserted in litigation brought by student victims of campus crime (Smith and Fossey, 1995).

There are four potential grounds for successful suits in this area. Three of these involve duties that colleges and universities may owe their students. The first is a duty to warn about known crime risks. The second is a duty to provide reasonably adequate security protection. Courts across the country now have clearly established that colleges owe their students these two duties, and legislation at both state and federal levels has further cemented the obligation to disclose foreseeable risks.

The third is a duty to screen employees and, perhaps in some circumstances, other students for crime risks. The fourth ground involves contractual liability; those who manage the institution must avoid creating additional, higher guarantees of protection than they can actually deliver. The remainder of this chapter will flesh out these four areas of hazard for the institutional administrator.

Warning of Known Risks

In 1984 the California Supreme Court decided the case of *Peterson* v. *San Francisco Community College District* and established a landmark precedent. The case involved a student who was assaulted and injured by a man who jumped from behind foliage along a stairway at a campus parking lot. After the attack the victim learned that the college had known of prior similar attacks in the same location. While the college had stepped up security patrols after the earlier attacks, the institution had not publicized the incidents or otherwise warned others. The court ruled the college was liable for the student's injuries because it had failed to give her a timely warning of the known risk.

In 1986, nineteen-year-old Jeanne Clery was raped and strangled in her dormitory room at Lehigh University. Again, the issue of prior but unpublicized crimes emerged. The parents of the dead student began a nationwide campaign to publicize the campus crime problem, and due largely to their efforts, *USA Today* urged in a 1989 editorial series that colleges be required to "open the books" on campus crime. The newspaper charged that "most" colleges conceal crime information to avoid adverse publicity ("Open the Books," 1989).

Soon state legislatures began adopting statutes requiring colleges to make crime statistics available, and in 1990 and 1991 Congress enacted the Student Right-to-Know and Campus Security Act, which requires every college and university receiving federal funds to make an annual report of crime statistics and other information about security operations to students and employees. (This federal legislation is discussed in detail in Chapter Three.)

Providing Adequate Campus Security

In recent years the courts have borrowed a doctrine from the field of law known as *landlord and tenant* to require that colleges and universities provide reasonably adequate security protection for their students. Failure to do so amounts to legal negligence, the decisions have held, and students injured as a result may sue for their losses to property and person.

Two factors are necessary for an institution to be held liable under this sort of negligence theory. First, it must have been foreseeable that the crime could occur, either because of a history of prior crimes in the area, or other factors of obvious danger. Second, if the crime was foreseeable, the institution must have failed to provide reasonable security measures to protect the victim. This begs the question of how much protection is reasonable. In a lawsuit, the jury's verdict will ultimately answer both questions: was the crime foreseeable, and was the provided security reasonable given the existing risk?

What factors are considered in deciding reasonableness? Such things as lights, locks, fences, gates, and the number, training, and deployment of police officers and security guards obviously are involved. Also implicated are the design and maintenance of physical facilities in order to eliminate or minimize dangerous places, and even modifications to academic programs so that classes, laboratories, and other activities are not required in isolated places or at dangerous hours, and that residence halls, cafeterias, and parking lots are safely accessible at all times.

The case of *Miller* v. *State of New York,* a 1984 decision by New York's highest court, illustrates the issues involved. The victim was a nineteen-year-old junior at a state university who was confronted in the laundry room of her residence hall at six o'clock one morning by an intruder holding a large butcher knife. The man marched her, blindfolded and at knife point, through an unlocked outer door of the dormitory basement, back into the building through another unlocked door and then upstairs to a third floor room where he raped her twice under threat of mutilation or death if she made noise. The assailant then took her back downstairs and outside to a parking lot, where he fled. He was never identified.

In her suit against the university, the young woman showed a history of crime on the campus. Prior to her attack strangers had been common in dormitory hallways, and there had been reports to campus security of men being found in the women's bathrooms. The plaintiff herself had twice complained to dormitory staff about nonresidents loitering in the building, and the campus newspaper had published reports of various crimes in the dormitories on the campus, including armed robbery, burglaries, trespass, and another rape. She showed that despite this history, the institution left all ten dormitory doors unlocked at all hours.

The New York court analogized the college to a landlord, and held it to the same duty that any landlord owes a tenant: to keep the premises in a reasonably safe condition, which includes a duty to maintain minimal security measures against foreseeable dangers. The university had breached that duty, the court held, upholding the jury's award of $400,000 to the student.

Crime history is not the only way to establish legal foreseeability. Other evident dangers will be sufficient. In a Massachusetts campus rape case, the victim established foreseeability by showing a quantum of contributing factors. Among them were that the campus was close to transportation lines leading to downtown Boston; college policies allowed male guests to stay overnight in women's dormitories; dormitory locks could readily be opened with credit cards or knives; fences around the campus were inadequate and gates were left unlocked; and although two guards were on night duty when she was attacked, there was no oversight system to ensure they were actually patrolling. The latter was an important point because the attack had lasted from sixty to ninety minutes, ranging over much of the campus, without detection. The final verdict included a personal judgment for $175,000 against the college's vice-president for operations, whose duty it was to oversee security operations (*Mullins* v. *Pine Manor College*, 1983).

Screening for Criminals

Do colleges and universities have a duty to screen employees and students in order to discover dangerous people? This is an emerging area of liability involving other sorts of businesses—primary and secondary schools, apartment complexes, even private security guard agencies. It can be expected to impinge upon college and university operations in coming years.

The only appellate case involving the screening of students is *Eiseman* v. *State of New York* (1987), in which a college knowingly admitted a parolee from a state prison. The admission was made as part of an experimental program to provide college opportunities for disadvantaged persons. After being taken to an off-campus party by unsuspecting students who had befriended him, the parolee went on a bloody rampage of murder and rape that left two other students dead and one maimed. After the attack it was learned that the parolee had a long, ugly history of heroin abuse, violent attacks, and two penitentiary sentences. College officials, knowing he was a convict, had made no effort to learn whether he might pose a risk. The jury held the college negligent and awarded more than $360,000 to the family of one of the slain students, but New York's highest court overturned the verdict, declaring that because the parole board—the "experts"—had decided the man was ready to return to society, the college could not be expected to do better. While the college ultimately won the case, it cannot be certain that other courts would reach the same conclusion in later cases, particularly where colleges know they are dealing with convicted felons.

Probably greater liability risks arise with the hiring, assignment, and retention of campus employees—especially those who will have master keys, or access to dormitories or other places where students may be especially vulnerable. The law recognizes that employers have a duty to take reasonable steps to ensure they are not deploying dangerous employees (Smith, 1993).

Contractual Theories: Making It Worse

Even though the law itself may impose no duty of protection from crime in a given situation (as, for instance, where the crime was not foreseeable, or where the institution has taken adequate security steps), it is possible for a college or university to create a higher duty for itself by its own actions. If it voluntarily guarantees certain security services but does not actually provide them, or guarantees safety, it may be held to the higher standard under the theory that the additional obligation is part of the contract between the institution and the student or employee.

In the case of students, assurances that might create this sort of liability can sometimes be found in the wording of college catalogues, promotional materials, housing contracts, and the like. The courts may construe promises of security to be contractual guarantees by the institution, as a seller of services, to the student as a buyer in the marketplace. The case of *Nieswand* v. *Cornell University* (1988) involved a freshman girl who was fatally shot, along with her roommate, in their residence hall room by a rejected suitor of the roommate. In their suit, the parents of the dead student pointed to two university publications that stated that residence halls were kept locked at night—a fact that was pertinent because the killer, armed with a rifle, had walked into the residence hall when it was supposed to have been locked. After the court handling the case ruled that the issue could go to a jury, the university settled the claim before trial for $200,000 ("Parents of Slain Student . . . ," 1989).

At the bottom line, administrators should take steps to assure that university publications do not make well-meaning but superfluous or inflated guarantees of safety or security. If the institution offers the assurance, it may have to live with the obligation.

Some Limitations: When Colleges Are Not Liable

The duties discussed in this chapter are subject to several important limitations in the realm of *who* and *where*. The duties of disclosure, reasonable security, and screening are not owed by a college or university to everyone in the general public. They are owed only to those people with whom the institution has what the law calls a *special relationship*—students, employees and others who come onto the campus at the institution's invitation to use campus facilities or programs that are open to them. Generally, however, trespassers or casual entrants on the premises are owed no such duties (Smith, 1992).

In like manner, the courts have been unwilling to impose liability upon colleges and universities in various sorts of situations where the institutions have little ability to protect against the risks. For example, the courts have not, thus far, extended the duty of security protection to off-campus sites. In *Donnell* v. *California Western School of Law* (1988), a California court of appeals held that a college's duty of protection did not extend to parking places on a city street immediately adjoining the school's building, even though there had been previous attacks there and the institution provided no parking of its own. The case involved a law student who was stabbed by a robber as he walked back to his car after studying late in the library. The court said that because the school did not own the city sidewalk it could not control it, and therefore the school owed no duty to protect its students on it. A similar result came in a West Virginia case involving a bar frequented by students (*Hartman* v. *Bethany College*, 1991).

On the other hand, it has been suggested that in some future cases colleges and universities may be held liable for failure to warn of foreseeable risks at off-campus sites that are an integral part of campus operations and are regularly used and relied upon by the campus community (Smith, 1992). There are implications here for off-campus housing (especially where the institution furnishes information about it), restaurants and bars, and the like.

Conclusion

There is no ignoring it. Colleges and universities—and even individual administrators—run a real risk of being held legally responsible for some of the victimizations occurring on their campuses. Informed, ameliorative steps must be taken. Campus decision makers should be familiar with the relevant principles of liability being applied in the courts, and take the indicated steps to reduce the risk of being sued. These steps will bring with them the avoidance of unwanted, negative publicity about the institution. More important, they will save lives.

References

"Open the Books on Campus Crime." *USA Today,* Nov. 13, 1989, p. 10A.

"Parents of Slain Student Settle Suit Against Cornell." *Chronicle of Higher Education,* Sept. 28, 1989, p. A2.

Smith, M. C. "Vexatious Victims of Campus Crime: Student Lawsuits as Impetus for Risk Management." *Journal of Security Administration,* 1992, *15,* 5–15.

Smith, M. C. "Revisiting Campus Insecurity: A Broader Brush is Essential." *Journal of Law and Education,* 1993, *22,* 189–196.

Smith, M. C., and Fossey, R. *Crime on Campus: Legal Issues and Campus Administration.* Phoenix, Ariz.: Oryx Press, 1995.

Legal References

Student Right-to-Know and Campus Security Act, Public Law No. 101–542 (1990), amended by Public Law No. 102–26, § 10(e) (1991); 20 U.S.C. § 1092(f).

Donnell v. California Western School of Law, 200 Cal. App. 3d 715, 246 Cal. Rptr. 199 (4th Dist. 1988).

Eiseman v. State of New York, 70 N.Y.S. 175, 518 N.Y.S.2d 608, 511 N.E.2d 1128 (1987).

Hartman v. Bethany College, 778 F. Supp. 286, (N.D. W. Va. 1991).

Miller v. State of New York, 62 N.Y.2d 506, 478 N.Y.S.2d 829, 467 N.E.2d 493 (1984); as to damages, see 110 A.D.2d 627, 487 N.Y.S.2d 115 (1985).

Mullins v. Pine Manor College, 389 Mass. 47, 449 N.E.2d 331 (1983).

Nieswand v. Cornell University, 692 F. Supp. 1464 (N.D. N.Y. 1988).

Peterson v. San Francisco Community College District, 685 P.2d 1193 (Cal. 1984).

MARGARET D. SMITH *is professor of education at the University of Southern Mississippi.*

Government now makes highly specific demands for disclosure of crime risks.

Campus Crime, College Policy, and Federal Laws and Regulations

Donald D. Gehring

Every student of higher education is aware that crime, and even violent crime, has always been a fact of campus life. In the 1800s a student was killed over a trout, a professor was killed at the University of Virginia, the president of a university in Mississippi was stabbed to death by a student, several students were shot at Miami University in Ohio, professors were stoned at the University of Georgia, and at the Universities of Missouri and North Carolina several students were stabbed and killed (Rudolph, 1990).

Policies and procedures to deal with campus crime have, until recently, always been left to administrators. In 1990 the United States Congress issued findings that the reported incidence of crime, particularly violent crime, on some college campuses has risen steadily in recent years and that although annual national campus violence surveys indicate that roughly 80 percent of campus crimes are committed by a student on another student and approximately 95 percent of the campus crimes that are violent are alcohol- and drug-related, there are currently no comprehensive data on campus crimes. The findings also showed that out of 8,000 postsecondary institutions participating in federal student aid programs, only 352 voluntarily provide crime statistics directly to the Federal Bureau of Investigation. Other institutions report data indirectly, through local police agencies or states, in a manner that does not permit campus statistics to be separated. In addition, several state legislatures have adopted or are considering legislation to require reporting of campus crime statistics and dissemination of security practices and procedures, but the bills are not uniform in their requirements and standards.

The congressional report went on to say that students and employees of institutions of higher education should be aware of the incidence of crime on

NEW DIRECTIONS FOR HIGHER EDUCATION, no. 95, Fall 1996 © Jossey-Bass Publishers campuses and policies and procedures to prevent crime or to report occur-rences of crime, and that applicants for enrollment at a college or university and their parents should have access to information about the crime statistics of that institution and its security policies and procedures. Further, although many institutions have established crime preventive measures to increase the safety of campuses, there is a clear need to encourage the development on all campuses of security policies and procedures; to standardize the reporting of crimes on campus; and to encourage the development of policies and proce-dures that address sexual assaults and racial violence on college campuses. (U.S. Congress, 1990.)

Armed with these findings, and in the face of a strong lobbying effort, Congress enacted the Campus Security Act as an amendment to the Student Consumer Information Act of 1976. The Student Consumer Information Act is a section of Title IV (student financial aid) of the Higher Education Act of 1965. Thus, the Campus Security Act applies to all institutions that receive stu-dent financial assistance under Title IV, which includes Pell Grants, Stafford Loans, PLUS and SLS funds, Federal Direct Student Loans, State Student Incentive Grants, Perkins Loans, SEOG and Work Study funds, and PAS and NEISP funding. Few public or private institutions are exempt from the require-ments of the Campus Security Act. In 1992 the Act was amended by the Sex-ual Assault Victim's Bill of Rights (*U.S. Code Cong. & Admin. News,* 1992), which greatly expanded the requirements of the Act. Generally, this protective policy law mandates that institutions receiving Title IV student aid funds annu-ally notify both students and employees of various programs, policies, and pro-cedures, as well as campus crime statistics. The law also directs the conduct of certain aspects of campus disciplinary hearings.

This protective policy law, mandating that adult students and employees annually be told where to report crimes, that victims can notify the police, and encouraging personal responsibility for safety has been viewed by some as a return to in loco parentis (Gehring, 1994). However, it is extremely important for administrators to know the requirements of the law and its regulations because failure to comply could result in tort liability suits, federal civil rights suits, and a loss of student aid funds.

The purpose of this chapter is to explain and analyze the requirements of the Campus Security Act as amended (from this point on whenever there is a reference to the Campus Security Act, it will include the Sexual Assault Vic-tim's Bill of Rights) as well as other protective policy laws and their regulations as they relate to campus crime. The chapter will also point out where the laws are unclear concerning an institution's responsibilities and the implications of some of the mandates. The best way to understand the requirements of these laws and their regulations, however, is to read them as they appear in the United States Code and the Code of Federal Regulations. In addition, when regulations are first published they appear in the *Federal Register* along with the comments and concerns of administrators in the field and explanatory responses and discussions from the Secretary of Education. These responses are helpful in understanding the meaning of a particular section or the secretary's position on the issues. Citations to all of these references appear at the end of this chapter and a reference or government documents librarian will be able to assist you in locating them. Reading these laws and regulations in the original is well worth the effort.

The Security Report

The requirements of the Campus Security Act have their genesis in a security report that each institution must develop and publish. The information required to be included in this document demands that a broad base of campus administrators and students be involved in the development and annual review of this publication. Campus programs, policies, procedures, and practices that must be included in the document dictate that, at least, personnel from campus housing, Greek life, counseling, judicial affairs, health services, physical plant, campus police, and academic affairs be included on the committee that puts the document together. Each unit of the institution not within a reasonable contiguous area of the main campus, such as a branch campus, must publish a separate report for its own campus.

Distribution of the Report. The regulations implementing the act specify that the security report be distributed annually to every student and employee "by appropriate publication and mailings through (i) direct mailings to each individual through the U.S. Postal Service, campus mail, or computer networks; and (ii) publications provided directly to each individual . . ." [34 C.F.R. § 668.47(b)(1)]. In discussing the distribution of the report in the *Federal Register* the secretary stated that "the regulations have been changed to clarify the methods of distribution that are to be used to *ensure individual delivery* of the security report." The secretary noted that institutions were free to use any method enumerated in the regulations such as the U.S. Postal Service, campus mail, computer networks, or "providing the report directly to each individual (*by hand-delivery*)" (emphasis added, 59 Fed. Reg. 22317, Apr. 29, 1994).

Neither the Campus Security Act statute nor its implementing regulations state that institutions must "ensure individual delivery" of the security report, yet the Secretary of Education is very clear in his discussion that that is what is expected. This is similar to the Drug Free Schools and Communities Act Amendments of 1989 (20 U.S.C. § 1145), which simply stated that the information required under the amendments be distributed annually to each student and employee, yet the Secretary of Education said in his discussion in the *Federal Register* (Aug. 16, 1990, p. 33595) that institutions must "ensure" that the information is distributed to each student and employee. This is certainly a much more demanding standard than the government imposed on the distribution of the Family Educational Rights and Privacy Act (FERPA). The more reasonable regulations of FERPA only require that the information be provided "by any means that are reasonably likely to inform . . . students of their rights" [34 C.F.R. § 99.7 (c)].

The secretary's comments also appear to require that if the security report is included in other publications provided directly to students, they must be "hand-delivered" (59 Fed. Reg. 22317, Apr. 29, 1994).

Another aspect of the distribution requirement that administrators may have missed because it was not a part of the proposed regulations involves prospective students and employees. Institutions are required to inform every prospective student and every prospective employee of the availability of the report and give each a copy of the summary of the contents of the report and the opportunity to request a copy of the full report. Of course, if they ask for a copy of the Security Report they must be provided with one [34 C.F.R. § 668.47 (b)(2)]. Prospective students (employees) are defined as individuals who have contacted the institution "for the purpose of requesting information concerning admission (employment) to (with) the institution" [34 C.F.R. § 668.41 (b) and 34 C.F.R. § 668.47 (f)]. It may be less burdensome to simply provide prospective students and employees with the entire report rather than printing two separate publications.

Information to Be Included in the Security Report. The security report must contain information on a variety of policies, programs, practices, and procedures related to crime prevention generally and sexual offenses specifically. Statistics on campus crimes must also be provided for the "three calendar years preceding the year in which the report is disclosed" [34 C.F.R. § 668.47 (b) (2)(iii)]. Reports are due on September first each year. Thus, the report due on September 1, 1996 should contain crime statistics covering the calendar years 1993, 1994, and 1995.

Institutional General Crime Policies

Probably the most important policy statement contained in the security report is that outlining the procedures and facilities for reporting crimes and other emergencies and those to whom the reports should be made. The regulations specify that "the title of each person or organization to whom students and employees should report criminal offenses . . ." [34 C.F.R. § 668.47(a)(1)] of murder, sexual offenses, aggravated assault, robbery, burglary, and motor vehicle theft must also be included in the report. These individuals are defined as "campus security authority" for purposes of the act [34 C.F.R. § 668.47(f)].

The security report also must contain institutional policies with respect to responding to reports of crimes as well as policies designed to encourage accurate and prompt reporting of crimes to campus police and other appropriate law enforcement units. The report must, in addition, contain the institution's policies "concerning security of and access to campus facilities, including campus residences . . ." [34 C.F.R. § 668.47(a)(2)]. Thus, institutions should include in the report when academic, administrative, and residential buildings are opened and when they are locked and the visitation policy for residence halls. Once the policy for locking buildings is established, it must be adhered to. The regulations define the term *campus* to include "any building or property owned or controlled by a student organization recognized by the institution" [34 C.F.R. § 668.47(f)(2)]. Thus, the regulations require that institutions also include security measures and access to private property owned by recognized student groups. Off-campus faculty clubs would not be included in the definition of *campus* and therefore security measures and access need not be reported unless the club is owned or controlled by the institution.

Institutions must also have a policy included in the report "concerning the monitoring and recording through local police agencies of criminal activity in which students engaged at off-campus locations of student organizations recognized by the institution, including student organizations with off-campus housing facilities" [34 C.F.R. § 668.47(a)(7)]. Administrators need to be aware that this includes criminal activity occurring not only at off-campus housing locations, but also at other off-campus locations of student organizations. For example, if a club team were to compete at a local city park and underage members were arrested for drinking after the contest, the regulations would seem to require that activity to be monitored and recorded. It is interesting that this monitoring and recording only pertains to student organizations but not to recognized faculty organizations.

The enforcement authority of security personnel and their working relationship with other police agencies as well as their arrest authority must also be delineated in the report.

Institutional policies related to the possession, use, and sale of alcoholic beverages and illegal drugs must be included in the security report as well as statements of policy regarding the enforcement of underage drinking laws and federal and state drug laws. This is a troublesome requirement for several reasons. The requirement goes well beyond the Drug Free Schools and Communities Act Amendments of 1989, which only required that institutions have standards of conduct that prohibit the unlawful possession, use, or distribution of illicit drugs or alcohol [34 C.F.R. § 86.100(a)(1)]. The Campus Security Act requires institutions to have a policy regarding enforcement of state and federal law. Colleges and universities should have standards of conduct for which they hold students accountable, but what should their policy be for enforcement of state and federal laws? Can they enforce the law? If private institutions engage in a policy of enforcing state law, are they engaged in state action and therefore required to provide Constitutional protection? Would a policy of notifying law enforcement agencies of violations of state underage drinking laws satisfy the requirement? Suppose security personnel do not have arrest authority?

Since the plain language of the regulations only requires that institutions have a policy regarding enforcement of state and federal laws, institutions may simply want to state that violations of state and federal law occurring on campus will be reported to the appropriate law enforcement authority.

Institutional General Crime Prevention Programs

Two types of programs are required to be described under the general crime prevention part of the Act (specific sexual offense programs will be covered later) and listed in the security report. The law and the regulations require that institutions describe the type and frequency of programs detailing campus security procedures and practices and encouraging students and employees to assume responsibility for their own security and the security of others. The security report must also contain a description of crime prevention programs as well as "any drug or alcohol-abuse programs required" [34 C.F.R. § 668.47(a)(11)] under the Drug Free Schools and Communities Act Amendments of 1989. This latter requirement may be met by cross-referencing the Drug Free Schools statement.

Neither the law nor the regulations say that institutions must have such programs. The plain language of the law simply says that they must describe the programs they have. This is quite different from the Drug Free Schools and Communities Act Amendments of 1989, which specifically describe what a higher education institution's drug prevention program must include (34 C.F.R. § 86.100). However, the Secretary of Education has interpreted Section 485(f) of the law, requiring "a description of the type and frequency of programs . . ." to mean that Section 485(f) "requires an institution to *provide* educational programs . . ." (emphasis added, 59 Fed. Reg. 22317, Apr. 29, 1994). The Secretary of Education thus equates the verb *describe* to the verb *provide*. Although institutions will want to provide educational programs, this is simply another example of bureaucratic overzealousness.

Statistics Required to Be Published in the Security Report

The statistics that must be included in the security report are of three major types. First, statistics on the occurrence of the "Big Six"—murder, robbery, aggravated assault, burglary, motor vehicle theft, and sexual offenses, forcible and nonforcible. These crimes are each defined in the appendix to the regulations (34 C.F.R. § 668, App. E). Murder requires a willful (not negligent) act; the elements of robbery include taking of property by force, threat of force or violence, or putting the victim in fear; aggravated assault generally requires an intention to do great bodily harm, usually with a weapon, but it is not necessary for injury to result; burglary is breaking and entering into a structure to commit a felony or theft; and motor vehicle theft includes the actual or attempted taking of a motor vehicle by an individual not having lawful access. Forcible sexual offenses include "any sexual act directed against another person, forcibly and/or against that person's will: or not forcible or against the person's will where the victim is incapable of giving consent" (U.S. Department of Justice, 1992, pp. 21–22). This would encompass forcible rape, forcible sodomy, sexual assault with an object, and forcible fondling. Nonforcible acts are also included as sexual offenses and are defined as "unlawful, nonforcible sexual intercourse" such as incest and statutory rape (nonforcible sexual intercourse with someone under the age of consent) (U.S. Department of Justice, 1992, p. 22).

Note that the definition of forcible sexual offenses includes acts "not forcibly against the person's will where the victim is incapable of giving consent because of his/her youth or because of his/her temporary or permanent mental or physical incapacity" (U.S. Department of Justice, 1992, pp. 21–22). In many states an individual under the influence of alcohol or drugs is considered incapable of giving consent. Students need to understand this definition of forcible rape, forcible sodomy, and forcible fondling, and the state law on consent. Thus, while an institution's statistics need only list the occurrence of sexual offenses, students should be provided with an explanation of what constitutes forcible rape.

Administrators should be aware that reporting the occurrence of one of the "Big Six" crimes does not require an arrest or a conviction, but only the degree of certainty that would lead police to conclude the crime did occur. The Secretary of Education has suggested that administrators refer to the *Unfounded Complaints* section of the Uniform Crime Reporting (UCR) Handbook published by the U.S. Department of Justice (59 Fed. Reg. 22317, Apr. 29, 1994). Certainly a written report or complaint seems to be a minimum prerequisite to indicate the occurrence of the crime. Although some would debate when to count an occurrence, it should be remembered that these statistics only need to be reported once a year in the security report, thereby generally providing ample time to verify an occurrence.

The second type of statistic that must be included in the security report is the number of actual arrests on campus for liquor law violations, drug abuse violations, and weapons possessions. Recall that institutions must have "a statement of policy regarding . . . the enforcement of State underage drinking laws" [34 C.F.R. § 668.47(a)(10)] and "enforcement of Federal and State drug laws" [34 C.F.R. § 668.47(1)(11)]. Under the Drug Free Schools and Communities Act only "standards of conduct" that prohibit unlawful possession, use, or distribution of alcohol or illicit drugs are required. Having a standard of conduct is quite different from a policy regarding the enforcement of state and federal law.

The regulations also require the inclusion of statistics in the security report concerning the number of murders, forcible rapes, and aggravated assaults that "manifest evidence of prejudice based on race, religion, sexual orientation, or ethnicity" [34 C.F.R. § 668.47(a)(6)(ii)]. The same type of statistics must be kept on liquor laws, drug abuse, and weapons violations [34 C.F.R. § 668.47(a)(8)(ii)]. Although examples of the crimes of murder, forcible rape, and aggravated assault manifesting prejudice seem apparent, it is difficult to conceive how liquor laws and drug abuse violations can manifest prejudice based on race, religion, sexual orientation, or ethnicity.

Reporting Crimes to the Campus Community

One of the most significant aspects of the Campus Security Act is the requirement that the institution notify the campus community of the occurrence of the "Big Six"—murder, forcible rape, robbery, burglary, aggravated assault, and motor vehicle theft. Not every occurrence of one of these crimes needs to be reported. The regulations specify that while the notice should be timely in order to put students and employees on notice and prevent similar crimes from occurring, it need only be given if campus authorities consider the particular crime to represent a threat to students and employees. Thus, the institution would probably want to post notices concerning a rape in which the perpetrator hid in the bushes and attacked the victim during the early morning hours; however, the institution might decide not to notify the campus where a student reports her car is stolen, explaining that her roommate took her car keys and drove her automobile to town without her knowledge or permission.

Because landowners (colleges and universities) have a legal duty to warn those who come upon the land to do business with the landowner (students and others) of foreseeable crimes, complying with the campus notice requirement is a good risk management practice (American Law Institute, 1965, § 344). Landlords have a similar duty (American Law Institute, 1965, § 314A) to their tenants (resident students). The public relations arguments against notifying the campus or minimizing the annual statistical reports are simply not valid. Besides being a violation of law and sending the wrong message to students, these arguments lack rationality. The fact is that no segment of our society is free of crime, and by notifying the community of the occurrence of crimes on campus, and publishing its crime statistics, the institution is letting everyone know that it is aware of the extent of crime on campus, cares about its students and employees, and is actively attacking the problem.

The regulations are very confusing on the issue of who needs to make reports to the campus community. The regulations provide that reports shall be made of the "Big Six" crimes that are considered a threat and are "reported to campus security authorities *as identified under the institution's current campus policies* pursuant to paragraph (a)(1) of this section or local police agencies" [34 C.F.R. § 668.47(e), emphasis added]. Paragraph (a)(1) is the policy statement in which the institution specifies to whom students and others should report criminal actions or other emergencies. As noted earlier, these individuals and organizations must be identified by title. Thus, it appears from the plain language that only campus security authorities as identified under the institution's policy need to make the reports to the campus. However, after specifying that campus security authorities are those identified under the institution's policy, the department then goes on to define *campus security authority* as more than that and includes the campus law enforcement unit and "an official of an institution who has significant responsibility for student and campus activities, but does not have significant counseling responsibilities" [34 C.F.R. § 668.47(f)].

As confusing as this is, I would suggest that the institutional policy identify the campus police as the organization to which to report all criminal actions and let that organization make reports to the campus. I would also be sure to include *counseling students* as part of the position description of residence life staff.

The Sexual Assault Victim's Bill of Rights Amendment

The Campus Security Act was amended by the Sexual Assault Victim's Bill of Rights (P.L. 102–325) in 1992. The amended law and implementing regulations require that additional information, policies, and procedures specifically related to sexual offenses be included in or with the security report.

Sexual Offense Prevention Programs. The first requirement, and appropriately so, is that institutions provide a statement concerning programs to prevent sexual offenses from occurring in the first place. Institutions must describe educational programs "to promote the awareness of rape, acquaintance rape, and other sex offenses" [34 C.F.R. § 668.47(12)(i)]. As mentioned earlier, the Secretary of Education has stated that he interprets "to describe" as "to have"; thus, institutions may not "describe" programs as not existing, but must actually provide educational programs.

Campus Procedures in Response to Sexual Offenses. Institutions must also include in or with the security report "procedures *students* should follow if a sex offense occurs . . . " [34 C.F.R. § 668.47(12)(ii), emphasis added], including whom to contact, to whom the offense should be reported, and why it is important to preserve evidence. Although this procedure and other information specifically targets students and never mentions employees, I would suggest that institutions also include procedures for employees to follow. In some instances the procedures may differ and employees should know what to do if they are victims of a sexual offense on campus. The requirement of listing the person to contact to make a report is redundant with the requirement in the Campus Security Act to list "procedures and facilities for students and others to report criminal actions and other emergencies occurring on campus" [34 C.F.R. § 668.47(a)(1)]. However, it may be a good idea to be redundant when communicating with students.

Disciplinary procedures may need to be modified and listed in or with the security report. Administrators should be sure that other publications containing disciplinary procedures are modified as well. The regulations require a "clear statement" that the accuser and the accused are both entitled to have others present during the hearing. This regulation does not say that attorneys must be permitted into the hearing if the normal practice is not to do so, but only that both sides are entitled to have others present. Neither does the use of the phrase "to have others present" seem to contemplate representation.

Administrators at public institutions should be aware that the due process requirements of the Fourteenth Amendment demand "fundamental fairness." While there is no general right to counsel in disciplinary hearings, if the institution allows one side to have counsel present, then due process would require that the other side also be allowed counsel; and if the university proceeded through counsel, then the accused should be allowed representation by counsel (*French* v. *Bashful,* 1969). Finally, if the student is being charged with a sexual offense off campus as well as in the campus disciplinary system, the student should be allowed to have counsel present for advice but not representation (*Gabrilowitz* v. *Newman,* 1978).

It must also clearly state in or with the security report the sanctions that may be imposed against those found to be responsible for either forcible or nonforcible sexual offenses. Sanctioning students who have committed sexual offenses must be very carefully thought out. In 1994 the U.S. Department of Education issued a notice of probable violation to the University of California, Santa Cruz, in which it stated that a one-year suspension imposed against a student found guilty of rape was "clearly inadequate" (Palomino, 1994). This finding, among others, was determined to constitute a probable violation of Title IX and as part of the Voluntary Resolution Plan, the Office of Civil Rights would require the University to place "the sanction and a coded notation indicating the basis for the sanctions . . . on the student's official transcript" (U.S. Department of Education, 1994, p. 4) for any student suspended or dismissed for rape, sexual assault, or serious sexual harassment.

Finally, institutions must include a clear statement that both the accused and accuser shall be informed of the outcome of the hearing for any sexual offense. Although this section of the law did not amend the Family Educational Rights and Privacy Act (FERPA) (20 U.S.C. § 1232g, 34 C.F.R. § 99), the regulations simply state that "compliance with this subsection does not constitute a violation of the Family Educational Rights and Privacy Act" [34 C.F.R. § 668.47(12)(B)]. The regulations do specify that informing both parties of the outcome of the hearing means "only the institution's final determination with respect to the alleged sex offense and any sanction that is imposed against the accused" [34 C.F.R. § 668.47(12)(B)].

In notifying the accuser of the outcome, institutions would be well advised to do so in writing. As a part of this written notice there should be a statement, as required by FERPA, that the disclosure is being made as required by the Campus Security Act and on the condition that it may not be redisclosed to anyone else without the permission of the accused student [34 C.F.R. § 99.33(a)(1)]. Students who are informed of the outcome should also be warned that redisclosure to anyone else without the consent of the accused could result in a suit for violation of privacy or conspiracy to violate the accused's civil rights (Gehring, 1995).

Sexual Offense Victim Information. Information about assistance available to victims of sexual assaults must also be included in or with the security report. The information must include a notification of both on- and off-campus counseling, mental health, and other victim services as well as a statement that victims have the option of notifying local law enforcement authorities and that institutional officials will assist victims in contacting local authorities if the victim elects to do so.

The institution must also include a statement that it "will change a victim's academic and living situations *after an alleged* sex offense and of the options for those changes, if those changes are requested by the victim and are reasonably available" [34 C.F.R. § 668.47(a)(12)(v), emphasis added]. Faculty particularly need to understand that the only two prerequisites for changing a student's academic situation are a request by the victim of an alleged offense and reasonable availability. Where there is no other course section for the victim to transfer into, an independent study may be a reasonable alternative. Of course, where there is strong evidence that an alleged perpetrator's continued presence on the campus constitutes a threat to others, an interim suspension may be invoked pending a hearing (*Gardenhire* v. *Chalmers*, 1971). Institutions, as landlords, must be particularly careful where there is an alleged rape and the alleged perpetrator lives in a coed hall (*Nero* v. *Kansas State University*, 1993).

Relationship of Campus Security Act to FERPA

The Campus Security Act also amended the Family Educational Rights and Privacy Act (FERPA) to allow, but not require, institutions to notify the victims of crimes of violence of the outcome of disciplinary hearings [34 C.F.R. § 99.31(13)]. This is a specific amendment that only provides that institutions are *not prohibited* from disclosing the outcome. It is unlike the provision in the Sexual Assault Victim's Bill of Rights, which does not amend FERPA, but requires the disclosure of disciplinary outcomes to victims of sexual offenses. The outcome, which is not defined, would probably include, as it does in the notice to sexual assault victims, the final determination and the sanction. The same admonition about redisclosure should be provided to victims as discussed earlier. A crime of violence is defined as "(a) an offense which has as an element the use, attempted use, or threatened use of physical force against the person or property of another, or (b) any other offense that is a felony and that, by its nature, involves a substantial risk that physical force against the person or property of another may be used in the course of committing the offense" (18 U.S.C. § 16).

Students should also be made aware that the records of campus law enforcement units are not protected under FERPA and may be open to the public, including newspapers, under state open public records laws. Many local police records are also open under state public records laws. Campus disciplinary records, however, are specifically protected from disclosure under FERPA except for the two exceptions noted above (to victims of crimes of violence and sexual assaults) and in the state of Georgia (*The Red and Black Publishing Company, Inc.* v. *Board of Regents*, 1993).

Other Federal Laws

In addition to the Campus Security Act, students should be aware that Subtitle C (Section 403.02) of the Violent Crime Control and Law Enforcement Act of 1994 (P.L. 103–322) creates a federal civil rights cause of action for anyone who is a victim of a gender-motivated act of violence. The same definition for violence is used in this law as is used in the Campus Security Act—18 U.S.C. § 16. Under this law the act of violence need not result in criminal charges, prosecution, or conviction. The interesting aspect of this law is that it creates a civil course of action in which the standard of proof is a preponderance of evidence (more than half) rather than beyond a reasonable doubt as required for a criminal conviction. In addition, as a civil suit, the remedy can be compensatory as well as punitive damages (money!). Students who are victims of gender-motivated crimes of violence should be aware of this option to bring a civil suit.

Summary

The Campus Security Act as amended by the Sexual Assault Victim's Bill of Rights and other federal laws requires that institutions provide a great deal of information to students and employees. This information is somewhat complicated and crosses boundaries of student affairs, academic affairs, human resources, and general university administration. Only a well-coordinated effort can ensure not only compliance with the law, but safe conditions on campuses.

References

American Law Institute. *Restatement (Second) of Torts*. St. Paul, Minn.: American Law Institute, 1965.

Gehring, D. "Protective Policy Laws." In M. Coomes and D. Gehring (eds.), *Student Services in a Changing Federal Climate*. New Directions for Student Services, no. 68. San Francisco: Jossey-Bass, 1994.

Gehring, D. "Abreast of the Law." *NASPA Forum*, Nov. 1995, p. 4.

Palomino, J. *Office for Civil Rights: Docket No. 09–93–2141: Letter of April 29, 1994 to Karl Pister*. Washington, D.C.: U.S. Department of Education.

Rudolph, F. *The American College and University: A History*. Athens, Ga.: University of Georgia Press, 1990.

U.S. Code Cong. & Admin. News, Sept. 7, 1992, No. 7.

U.S. Congress. House. H. Doc. 101–883. 101st Cong., 2d sess., 1990.

U.S. Department of Education. *Office for Civil Rights: Docket No. 09–93–2141: Voluntary Resolution Plan*. Washington, D.C.: U.S. Department of Education, 1994.

U.S. Department of Justice. *Uniform Crime Reporting Handbook*. Washington, D.C.: U.S. Department of Justice, 1992.

Legal References

Drug Free Schools and Communities Act Amendments of 1989, 20 U.S.C. § 1145, implemented by 34 C.F.R. § 86 (see 55 Fed. Reg. 33580, Aug. 16, 1990 for comments).

Family Educational Rights and Privacy Act of 1974, 20 U.S.C. § 1232, implemented by 34 C.F.R. § 99.7(c).

Student Right-to-Know and Campus Security Act (as amended by the Sexual Assault Victim's Bill of Rights), 20 U.S.C. § 1092, implemented by 34 C.F.R. § 668.47 (see 59 Fed. Reg. 22303, Apr. 29, 1994 for comments).

Violent Crime Control and Law Enforcement Act of 1994, 42 U.S.C. § 13701 (P.L. 103–322, Sept. 13, 1994).

French v. *Bashful*, 303 F. Supp. 1333 (E.D. La. New Orleans 1969).

Gabrilowitz v. *Newman*, 5812 F.2d 100 (1st Cir. 1978).

Gardenhire v. *Chalmers*, 326 F. Supp. 1200 (D. Ks. 1971).

Nero v. *Kansas State University*, 861 P.2d 768 (Ks. 1993).

Red and Black Publishing Company, Inc. v. *Board of Regents*, 427 S.E.2d 257 (Ga. 1993).

DONALD D. GEHRING *is professor of higher education and student affairs and director of the higher education doctoral program at Bowling Green State University.*

Campus leaders need to consider both prevention and appropriate response.

Responding to Campus Rape: A Practical Guide for College Administrators

Richard Fossey, Michael Clay Smith

In movies and popular literature, college campuses are often portrayed as carefree havens of easy morality, where students and professors indulge in casual and harmless sexual relationships. Research studies, however, paint a very different picture of sexual behavior at colleges and universities. At some higher education institutions, college women run a one-in-five chance of experiencing an attempted or completed sexual assault, with freshman women being at greatest risk for rape. Far too often, college fraternities are involved in sexual misbehavior, occasionally even including sexual assault. Indeed, two popular movie comedies, *Animal House* and *Revenge of the Nerds,* portray fraternity men engaging in antics toward women which would probably be criminal offenses if they were actually to occur. Male varsity athletes often figure prominently in incidents of sexual misconduct, and research confirms that they are more likely than the average college male to be involved in various forms of rape.

Twenty years ago, few campus administrators spent much time dealing with campus-related rapes. Sexual misconduct became a police matter only on rare occasions, with most institutions preferring to handle rape allegations internally to avoid embarrassing individuals or the institution. Unfortunately, this policy often failed to provide rape victims with needed assistance and support; and perpetrators frequently escaped justice.

Reprinted from *Crime on Campus: Legal Issues and Campus Administration* by Michael Clay Smith and Richard Fossey. Used with permission of the American Council on Education and The Oryx Press, 4041 N. Central Ave., Suite 700, Phoenix, AZ 85012. (800) 279–6799.

Three developments have changed this scenario, however, and made sex crimes a central concern for most colleges and universities. First, federal laws—notably, the Ramstad Amendment, and the Student Right-to-Know and Campus Security Act—have forced higher education institutions to assume more responsibility for preventing sexual assaults. Second, courts have shown themselves more willing to hold institutions liable for sexual assaults that occur on college campuses. Third, higher education administrators, like society as a whole, are becoming more sensitive to the fact that the victims of sex crimes often suffer severe trauma, with long-term physical and psychological consequences. Campus decision makers are becoming increasingly aware that the atmosphere of learning and free inquiry which every college and university strives for requires a safe and secure environment for faculty and students.

Common Characteristics of Campus-Related Rape

It is clear that the number of campus-related rapes that are reported constitute only a fraction of all the rapes that actually occur. A Department of Justice study has estimated that actual rapes may number from three and one-half to nine times as many as are reported. Moreover, the reporting rate may be even lower when the victim is acquainted with the rapist. Studies have estimated that only one in a hundred acquaintance rapes gets reported to the police. Some studies have estimated that a college woman's chance of being sexually assaulted while she is a student is from 20 to 25 percent (Bohmer and Parrott, 1993). A recent study found that one in three college women had experienced nonconsensual or pressured sexual intercourse—either by physical force, through the influence of drugs or alcohol, or by psychological pressure (although many of these incidents might not fall within the legal definition of rape) (Finley and Corty, 1993).

Rape victims fail to report for many reasons. Among them are avoidance of embarrassment, concern that they will receive unsympathetic treatment from police and courts, fear of reprisal by the rapist, and lack of confidence that the police can apprehend the perpetrator. Alcohol is often a factor in campus-related rapes, and it seems likely that some victims fail to report because they blame themselves for having been under the influence of alcohol when the rape occurred.

There is no such thing as a typical campus rapist, but certain kinds of students figure more prominently in sex offenses than others. Fraternity members are more likely than non–fraternity members to engage in nonphysical pressure and to use drugs or alcohol as a means of facilitating sex, but they are no more likely than other campus males to use physical force (Boeringer, Shehan, and Akers, 1991). In addition to fraternity men, student athletes have a high propensity for committing campus-related rape, perhaps because of their privileged position on campus (Bohmer and Parrott, 1993). Although campus rapes take place in a variety of settings, they often occur at parties, especially fraternity parties, and alcohol is frequently a factor.

A high proportion of campus-related rapes involve female college students who are on their own for the first time (Finley and Corty, 1993). They may become rape victims partly because their inexperience caused them to fail to appreciate risks or to misread the danger in a social situation. Colleges and universities enroll large numbers of such women, and they should make a special effort to make them aware of the danger of both acquaintance and stranger rape, and, when such women reside on campus, to provide them with a safe and secure living environment.

The Ramstad Amendment and a University's Responsibility to Help Avert Sex Crimes on Campus

In 1992, Congress passed the Ramstad Amendment, which requires higher education institutions to adopt policies to prevent sex offenses and procedures to deal with sex offenses once they have occurred. The law specifies that the following areas will be addressed:

Education programs to promote awareness of rape, acquaintance rape, and
    other sex crimes
Institutional sanctions for sex offenses, both forcible and nonforcible
Procedures students should follow if they become a sexual assault victim,
    including who should be contacted, the importance of retaining evidence,
    and to whom the offense should be reported.

In addition, the Ramstad Amendment requires colleges to give sex-crime victims the same right as the accused to have others present during disciplinary proceedings. Moreover, the college must inform the accuser and the accused of the outcome of any on-campus disciplinary proceeding. Institutions are also required to notify the victim that she has the option of reporting the sexual assault to law enforcement authorities and that she will receive assistance from the institution in that process. Finally, the law requires campus authorities to notify sexual assault victims about available counseling services and options for changing academic schedules and living arrangements in the wake of a sexual assault.

Crime Reporting Obligations: The Student Right-to-Know and Campus Security Act of 1990

In 1990, Congress passed the Student Right-to-Know and Campus Security Act, which requires post-secondary institutions to collect information about campus crime and to publish it on an annual basis. Specifically, institutions are required to disseminate an "annual security report" to students and staff that contains the following information:

A statement of current campus policies for handling campus crimes or other emer-
    gencies, including procedures for receiving reports from students and employees

A statement of current policies for maintaining campus security, including security arrangements for campus housing and off-campus housing maintained by fraternities, sororities, or other student organizations

A statement of current policies concerning campus law enforcement, including the enforcement authority of campus security forces and their working relationship with state and local law enforcement agencies and policies that encourage prompt and accurate reporting of campus crimes to law enforcement authorities

A description of the type and frequency of programs designed to inform students and employees of campus security procedures and to encourage students and employees to take responsibility for their own safety and the safety of others

A description of programs designed to inform students and employees about crime prevention

A statement of policy concerning the monitoring and recording of criminal activity at off-campus student organizations, such as fraternities and sororities

A description of policies and procedures regarding possession, use, and sale of alcoholic beverages and illegal drugs

A description of available drug and alcohol abuse programs.

In addition, the annual security report must contain statistics on the occurrence of certain crimes during the current and two preceding school years. Specifically, higher education institutions must provide statistics on murder, forcible and non-forcible sex offenses, robbery, aggravated assault, burglary, and motor vehicle theft. Institutions must also report statistics concerning arrests for liquor law violations, drug abuse violations, and weapons possession.

Perhaps most importantly, the Student Right-to-Know and Campus Security Act requires post-secondary institutions to make timely reports to the campus community on major crimes that are considered to be a threat to other students or employees. The law requires not only that these reports be timely but that they be provided "in a manner . . . that will aid in the prevention of similar occurrences."

It is too early to tell whether the Campus Security Act will increase colleges' exposure to liability. It seems possible that the law's requirements will be cited by plaintiff crime victims as the standard of care, breach of which would form the basis for liability. For example, the law requires institutions to make timely reports of crimes that might constitute a danger to the campus community. A college that failed to publicize the presence of a serial rapist, to take one example, might face liability to a victim who could have taken precautions had she been informed that a dangerous sex offender was operating in her area. In other words, the Campus Security Act may have established a federally mandated "duty to warn" (Griffaton, 1993).

Institutional Liability for Campus Rapes

In recent years there have been a number of cases in which rape victims have sued institutions to collect money damages for, in a sense, helping to make the rape possible. Basically, institutions of higher education owe a duty to take precautions against foreseeable dangers, and to provide a reasonably safe environment for their students and employees (Bhirdo, 1989). If a college breaches that duty and if a rape occurs that might have been avoided through better security or warnings, the college may be subject to money damages.

In the 1984 case of *Peterson* v. *San Francisco Community College District,* the California Supreme Court held that a student could sue the college for injuries received in an attempted rape in a college parking lot. In that case the student maintained that the college had been on notice of previous assaults in the parking lot, and had failed to warn students. She also accused the college of increasing the danger of criminal assault by failing to trim the foliage around the parking lot.

A similar result had come a year earlier in *Mullins* v. *Pine Manor College* (1983), a Massachusetts case. A female student was raped on campus by an unidentified assailant who was never apprehended. On the night of the rape two guards were on duty at the 400-student school. The victim was awakened in her dormitory room by an intruder who forced her out of the building, across the courtyard, and off campus for a time. The entire incident, including the rape, lasted for more than an hour.

The *Mullins* court held that parents, students, and the general community had an enforceable expectation, fostered in part by the college itself, that reasonable care would be exercised to protect resident students from foreseeable harm. Although there had been no incidents of violent crimes on campus in the years prior to the attack, the college was in a metropolitan area, and the director of student affairs had warned students during freshman orientation of the dangers inherent in being only a short distance from bus and train lines that led directly to Boston. The court therefore held that the risk of a criminal act was not only foreseeable but actually had been foreseen by the school. The opinion noted that the concentration of young people, especially young women, on a college campus, "creates favorable opportunities for criminal behavior."

Another dormitory rape case, *Miller* v. *State of New York* (1984), also illustrates a university's obligation to provide adequate security measures for students. A 19-year-old junior at the State University of New York at Stony Brook was confronted by an intruder armed with a large butcher knife in the laundry room of her residence hall at six o'clock one morning. He blindfolded her and marched her, at knife point, through an unlocked outer door of the dormitory basement, back through another unlocked door of the building, and then upstairs to a third floor room where she was raped twice under threat of mutilation or death if she made noise. The man then led her back downstairs and outside to a parking lot. He fled and was never identified.

At trial the victim was able to show that prior to her attack strangers had been common in dormitory hallways, and reports to campus security of men in the women's bathroom had been made. The student had herself twice complained to dormitory supervisors about nonresidents loitering in the building. The campus newspaper had published accounts of many crimes in the dormitories at the school, including armed robbery, burglaries, trespass, and another rape. Even so, all ten dormitory doors were kept unlocked at all hours.

The court held that the college was in essence a landlord and it owed the same duty any landlord owed a tenant: the premises must be kept in a reasonably safe condition—including "minimal security measures" against foreseeable dangers. The court ruled that failure to lock the doors breached this duty.

A university's representations of dormitory safety led to one suit alleging deceit and misrepresentation by the institution (*Duarte v. State of California*, 1979). After a female student was sexually assaulted and murdered in her dormitory room at California State University, the victim's mother claimed that she had relied on the university's representations and the dormitory's appearance of safety and security when she decided to let her daughter live there. She complained that the school had been aware of increased violence on the campus, but had chosen to ignore it. In holding that the suit could proceed, the court noted that the representation that the dormitories were safe was made by university officials "with presumed superior knowledge" of dangers.

Of course, colleges are not automatically liable when a student is sexually assaulted. For example, a federal district court ruled that Bethany College, a private institution in West Virginia, was not liable for the reported rape of a seventeen-year-old student that occurred at an off-campus bar (*Hartman v. Bethany College*, 1991). The student, who was below the legal drinking age in West Virginia, met her assailants at the bar, where she was given alcoholic beverages. Later she was taken to another location and raped.

Colleges are not required to supervise students after they leave the campus, the court ruled, nor are they required to advise students of state laws. The court rejected the plaintiff's argument that because of her minority the college stood *in loco parentis* to her. "It is not reasonable to conclude today that seventeen-year-old college students necessarily require parental protection and supervision," the court said. "If they did, society might place many more limitations upon the ability of a minor to attend college than currently exist" (*Hartman v. Bethany College*, p. 294).

Likewise, in another case involving underage drinking, the California Court of Appeals ruled that the University of California at Berkeley was not legally responsible when a first-year student was sexually assaulted by four university football players in a coed dormitory (*Tanja H. v. Regents of the University of California*, 1991). The assaults took place after a dormitory drinking party.

The victim argued that a shattered light bulb on the landing in a stairwell was a contributing factor, along with the fact that men and women resided together on the same dormitory floor. However, in the court's view, there was no evidence that better lighting on the stairwell landing would have prevented the attacks, some of which occurred in dormitory rooms. Nor was there any evidence that segregating the sexes on different dormitory floors would have deterred the assaults, since, as the court pointed out, the assailants knew how to use the stairs.

In addition, although several courts have recognized a university's obligation to protect students from a foreseeable danger of campus rape, at least one court refused to find such an obligation when the alleged rape did not occur during a university-sponsored activity. In *Leonardi v. Bradley University* (1993), an Illinois appellate court acknowledged that the school might owe a legal duty of care to students who were taking part in university-sponsored activities, because students would have the status of business invitees during such times. However, the court ruled that a late-night visit to a fraternity house did not make the victim a business invitee of the university.

Do colleges and universities have a duty to screen those coming on campus to discover dangerous persons? A New York court examined this question in *Eiseman v. State of New York* (1987). An admittee to an experimental program at the State University College at Buffalo designed to provide college opportunities for disadvantaged persons was a released convict from the state penitentiary. He was invited to an off-campus party by unsuspecting students who had befriended him. At the party, the parolee went on a bloody spree of murder and rape which left two other students dead and one seriously injured. It was later learned that the assailant had a long and ugly history of heroin abuse, violent attacks on others, and two penitentiary sentences. Even though they had known he was incarcerated when he applied for admission, college officials had made no effort to learn whether he might pose a risk to the college community.

The New York Court of Appeals reversed a verdict for the victim's family, declaring that because the parole board's experts had released the man into society, the college was not obligated to inquire into his history before accepting him into its student body.

However, *Nero v. Kansas State University* (1993) ruled that Kansas State University (KSU) might have a responsibility to protect students from another student who had been charged, but not convicted, of rape. In that case, a male student who resided in a coed dormitory was charged with raping a female student who lived in the same dormitory. Pending disposition of the criminal charges, KSU officials transferred the accused student to an all-male dormitory on the other side of campus.

Shortly thereafter, however, the academic school year ended; and the accused student moved to Goodnow Hall, another coed dormitory, the only KSU dormitory available to students attending intersession and summer school. Thirty-five days after he reportedly raped the first woman, the student was accused of sexually assaulting a second student in the basement of Goodnow Hall. He later plead guilty to raping the first student. In return, authorities dropped the sexual assault charge involving the second student.

The Goodnow resident sued KSU for negligence. She argued that the university had breached its duty of care to her by failing to protect her from a foreseeable assault. Her claims were dismissed by the trial court, but the Kansas Supreme Court reversed and ordered a trial. A majority of the court ruled that a factual issue existed concerning whether KSU used reasonable care in placing an accused rapist in a coed dormitory. In addition, the court ruled that there were factual issues concerning whether the second woman should have been warned of the danger that the accused rapist presented and whether adequate security measures had been taken to protect her.

From this line of cases certain themes emerge. First, higher education institutions have a responsibility to protect the campus community from foreseeable dangers, which means they should take special precautions in areas that are known to be dangerous. In addition, some cases have ruled that education institutions have a duty to warn students of any known danger of sexual assault. In general, colleges are held to the same standard of care imposed on landlords who know of dangerous conditions on their premises. Some courts have ruled that an institution's duty to protect students and staff from rape arises if the college or university knows about prior sexual assaults, but one court imposed liability on a college based in part on the fact that the institution knew that a campus crime might occur simply because the school was located in an urban area.

Recent federal legislation underscores the responsibility of colleges and universities to maintain safe campus environments. Institutions may now have a specific duty to warn based on the Campus Security Act, which requires colleges to give timely notice of criminal activity that may endanger staff or students. Institutions also have a statutory obligation under the Ramstad Amendment to provide crime awareness education to students, and this would seem to apply most forcefully for first-year women, who are at highest risk of rape.

Liability for Rapes Committed by Campus Employees

Colleges and universities may face an increased risk of liability if the individual who commits the rape is an employee. Courts are split with regard to whether employers are liable for an employee's sexual offenses. Some take the view that an employee who commits a serious criminal offense such as rape is not acting within the scope of his employment, and thus employers bear no responsibility for this kind of misconduct unless it occurred through negligent hiring or negligent supervision.

In Louisiana, an appellate court recently approved a judgment against Grambling State University in a suit involving a charge of rape against a Grambling student and summer employee (*Dismuke v. Quaynor,* 1994). The victim was a fifteen-year-old girl who was attending a summer sports program at Grambling. The accused assailant pled guilty to carnal knowledge of a juvenile, and a default judgment was entered against him in the girl's civil suit. She also sued Grambling, and a judgment was rendered against the university for $110,000.

Based on the facts of the case, the Louisiana Court of Appeals upheld the trial court's decision to hold Grambling vicariously liable for the incident. The court concluded that the assailant committed a wrongful act on Grambling's campus during normal class hours and almost immediately after the summer sport class had been dismissed early due to bad weather. It also found that the tort was committed while the perpetrator was engaged in an employment-related activity, even though he was probably "technically" off duty for the day.

College and university decision makers should note that Grambling was held vicariously liable for an employee's sexual misconduct without regard to the university's fault; and thus it is a departure from the general trend of case law in this area. As discussed above, higher education institutions have been held liable for rapes that occur on campus, but previously their liability has always hinged on a finding of negligence.

In addition to potential liability under state tort law, colleges and universities may also be exposed to money damages under Title IX of the Education Amendments of 1972 if a campus employee sexually assaults another staff member or a student. In *Franklin* v. *Gwinnett County Public Schools* (1992), the Supreme Court permitted a high school student to sue a Georgia school district for damages under Title IX, based on her accusation that a teacher had sexually harassed her by engaging in conduct that culminated in three acts of "coercive intercourse." Although the Court did not use the word "rape" to describe the student's allegations, it seems likely that rape of a student or campus worker by a college or university employee is actionable under Title IX, particularly if the employee was aided in his assault by his employment status (Vargyas, 1993).

Sex Crimes Against Children: Special Campus Concerns

Campus administrators should remember that colleges and universities are hosts not only to college-age students but to children and adolescents as well. Many colleges offer summer sports clinics and academic enrichment courses which attract children as young as elementary-school age. And of course, most institutions will enroll at least a few freshman students who are under the age of eighteen, which means they have the legal status of children in many states.

The presence of children on campus may impose special legal obligations on colleges and universities, obligations with which they may not be familiar. For example, all fifty states require educators to report incidents of child abuse that they learn about in the course of their professional duties, and many of these laws are broad enough to cover higher education employees as well as public school teachers and administrators. In most states, it is a criminal offense for mandated reporters to fail to report child abuse that they know about, and some states permit civil suits against persons who violate the child abuse reporting statutes. Thus it is essential for campus personnel who work with children to be thoroughly familiar with the child abuse reporting laws.

In addition, higher education authorities must take special care when they hire people who operate on-campus sports and academic programs for children. Unfortunately, some adults seek child-care employment in order to have opportunities to abuse children. Many states now require school districts and child-care agencies to conduct criminal background checks on prospective employees who will have contact with children (Davidson, 1985), and university counsel would be wise to review the legislation in their jurisdiction to determine whether these laws apply to their institutions' child-oriented programs.

Protecting the Campus

One study has provided an excellent checklist of potential problems for those evaluating the safety of campuses. Prepared by Dr. Leonard Territo of the University of South Florida, it identifies the following considerations: (1) surveillance of problem locations, which are sites of previous assaults, indecent exposure, robberies, purse snatchings, and the like, and which will warrant special attention from security guards, escort services, extra lighting, emergency telephones, and so forth; (2) lighting standards to assure that nationally recommended illumination amounts are provided, and that burned-out lights or reduced usage of existing lighting to conserve energy are not creating a danger; (3) grounds-keeping responsibilities, to avoid shrubbery and hedges of sufficient height or location to provide a hiding place for an assailant; (4) scheduling of classes, to avoid night classes in isolated locations; (5) emergency telephones, to assure that telephones are accessible after offices are closed and without need of coins at walking routes, parking lots, and recreation areas; (6) dormitory security, ensuring that protection exists even though coed dormitories are used and curfews are often a thing of the past; (7) arrangement of after-hours and weekend work so that isolated employees are not left in lonely areas; (8) rape prevention programs, to provide women beforehand with various rape prevention techniques; and (9) crime-prevention training for security personnel, so that expertise can be brought to bear in campus planning and programs (Territo, 1983).

Institutional Responsibility Following a Rape

In addition to developing preventive measures, universities have a responsibility to assist the victim after a rape occurs. Specifically, many student rape victims will seek medical assistance at the campus health clinic. The health care professionals who staff these clinics should be familiar with the psychological consequences of rape trauma and trained to safeguard the evidence necessary to obtain a criminal conviction. A victim may wish to change her housing situation because of the rape, and campus housing authorities should be prepared to make this accommodation quickly and with a minimum of fuss. Finally, some designated campus representative should inform the victim of internal grievance procedures as well as criminal and civil options, and this counseling should be supplemented with literature that outlines the victims' options for seeking redress and the campus services that are available to assist them.

Universities should also make sure that campus law enforcement officials have the expertise that is necessary to investigate and successfully prosecute these cases when they occur. Institutions that are too small to support a sophisticated crime investigation unit should make sure that local law enforcement authorities can step in quickly to conduct a rape investigation if the need arises.

Conclusion

Campuses have a duty to protect students from foreseeable criminal acts, including campus rapes. In general, courts have held that colleges have a duty to protect students from known dangers, including the danger of sexual assault. This duty may be breached by failing to provide adequate security or by failing to warn of recent criminal activity.

Even if colleges were inclined to sweep incidents of sexual misconduct under the rug, they are no longer free to do so. Moreover, piecemeal measures and half-hearted approaches will no longer suffice to deal with sexual harassment and sexual violence. Institutions must develop a comprehensive response, involving not only campus police, but also groundskeeping and maintenance departments, student services, medical staff, counselors, and housing personnel.

At a minimum, the following issues should be addressed:

• A rape awareness program, utilizing trained staff and literature, should be developed. The program should target the campus community's most vulnerable members—first-year college women—and the groups that are often prominent in sexual misconduct incidents—fraternities and student athletes. Victims should know where they can go for assistance, and potential aggressors should know the consequences if they use physical force, drugs, or alcohol to obtain sex. A rape awareness program should emphasize the part that alcohol plays in campus sexual aggression.

• A campus sexual harassment policy that complies with the Ramstad Amendment should be developed and disseminated. This policy should reflect the institution's expectations with regard to faculty-student liaisons and the penalties for sexual misconduct.

• A campus security plan should reflect the institution's efforts to prevent sexual assault. The plan should address lighting, shrubbery, police patrols, escort services, call boxes in isolated locations, and residence-hall security.

• A routine procedure should be put in place to notify the campus community about serious criminal activity that is likely to be an ongoing threat to students and employees. This is a requirement of the Student Right-to-Know and Campus Security Act.

• Campus disciplinary procedures should be reviewed to make sure they are adequate to address complaints about serious sexual misconduct. All persons who participate in campus adjudicatory proceedings should be trained and thoroughly understand their roles. The institution should develop a clear policy about which kinds of sexual offenses will be handled internally, and which will be turned over to the criminal authorities.

• Institutions should review their programs for elementary and secondary school students to make sure these students are adequately protected from sexual assaults. Campus employees who work with minor children should be trained in the requirements of the child abuse reporting laws and any laws that require criminal background checks for prospective child-care employees. Colleges and universities should make sure that their hiring procedures are adequate to prevent convicted child molesters from obtaining employment around children.

Finally, campus decision makers should understand that an effective program to prevent campus sex crimes is not something that can be put in place and then be forgotten. Sex crime awareness programs need to be offered on an annual basis, in order to educate first-time students, recently arrived international students, and new employees. Campus security must be constantly monitored for such problems as inadequate lighting, overgrown shrubbery, or careless dormitory security (see Appendix A). Institutional policies against sexual harassment should be reemphasized to faculty, employees and students on a regular basis so that everyone understands that these policies reflect institutional values and are not just empty words. In short, the task of protecting the campus community from sexual assaults and harassment must become an integral part of the institution's day-to-day mission of providing a safe and secure learning and working environment.

Appendix A:
General Campus Security Checklist

Perimeter

Is traffic flow through campus minimized?
Are fences adequate to discourage entry?
Is lighting adequate at entrances and on streets?

Students

Are crime statistics furnished students regularly?
Is there an emergency notification procedure?
Is there an escort system?
Are students disciplined for propping doors open or stuffing locks on doors?
Are drug and alcohol rules adequately enforced?
Does the institution screen for dangerous applicants?
Does it expel dangerous miscreants?
Are procedures in place for students to complain about security?

Is the campus community warned of any criminal activity that might present a danger to students and employees?

Are campus medical staff members trained to deal with rape trauma and to preserve evidence of rape?

Are rape victims informed of their right to file charges with campus or local police and are they given assistance in this process?

Does the university offer to change housing or academic arrangements for sex crime victims in appropriate circumstances?

Do campus staff members comply with child abuse reporting laws when a sex crime victim is a minor student?

Grounds and Buildings

Is shrubbery minimized?

Is lighting adequate at buildings and walkways?

Are lights monitored for burn-outs and failures?

Is master key control tight?

Are locks re-cored as needed?

Are emergency phones available in remote areas?

Do closed circuit televisions monitor remote places?

Policing

Is the number of patrol officers sufficient?

Are officers given adequate original and continuing training?

Are incident reports monitored by administration?

Are incident reports made available to campus press to enable appropriate publicity about ongoing crime activity?

Are officers required to verify their patrol patterns to make sure that dangerous areas are regularly monitored?

Housing

Are visitors regulated?

Do policies punish door propping and lock stuffing?

Are new employees screened?

Are police patrols adequate?

Does the institution enforce drug/alcohol rules?

Are deadbolt locks and peepholes provided?

Are keys changed periodically?

Are emergency phones accessible?

Is elevator access controlled?

Is there enough on-campus housing for all who want it?

Are students given choice of more secure dormitory?

Are there crime education programs for students, particularly first-year undergraduate women and newly arrived international students?

Are dormitory access points locked or otherwise secured?

Parking

Is parking safely accessible?

Are parking areas viewed by other people?

Are lots patrolled?

Are emergency phones in place?

Are night classes scheduled to avoid isolated classrooms?

References

Bhirdo, K. W. "Liability for Victimization of Students." *Journal of College and University Law,* 1989, *16,* 119.

Boeringer, S., Shehan, C., and Akers, R. "Social Contexts and Social Learning in Sexual Coercion and Aggression: Assessing the Contribution of Fraternity Membership." *Family Relations,* 1991, *40,* 58–64.

Bohmer, C., and Parrott, A. *Sexual Assault on Campus.* San Francisco: New Lexington Press, 1993.

Davidson, J. "Protection of Children Through Criminal History Record Screening, Well-Meaning Promises and Legal Pitfalls." *Dickinson Law Review,* 1985, *89,* 577.

Finley, C., and Corty, E. "Rape on Campus: The Prevalence of Sexual Assault While Enrolled in College." *Journal of College Student Development,* 1993, *34,* 113–117.

Griffaton, M. C. "Forewarned Is Forearmed: The Crime Awareness and Campus Security Act of 1990 and the Future of Institutional Liability for Student Victimization." *Case Western Reserve Law Review,* 1993, *43,* 525.

Territo, L. "Campus Rape: Determining Liability." *Trial,* Sept. 1983, 100–103.

Vargyas, E. J. "*Franklin* v. *Gwinnett County Public Schools* and Its Impact on Title IX Enforcement." *Journal of College and University Law,* 1993, *19,* 373.

Legal References

Dismuke v. *Quaynor,* 637 So.2d 555 (La. Ct. App. 1994).

Duarte v. *State of California,* 88 Cal. App. 3d 473, 151 Cal. Rptr. 727 (1979).

Eiseman v. *State of New York,* 70 N.Y.2d 175, 518 N.Y.S.2d 608 (1987).

Franklin v. *Gwinnett County Public Schools,* 506 U.S. 70 (1992).

Hartman v. *Bethany College,* 778 F.Supp. 286 (N.D. W. Va. 1991).

Leonardi v. *Bradley University,* 625 N.E.2d 431 (Ill. Ct. App. 1993).

Miller v. *State of New York,* 62 N.Y.2d 493, 478 N.Y.S.2d 829, 467 N.E. 493 (1984).

Mullins v. *Pine Manor College,* 449 N.E.2d 331 (Mass. 1983).

Nero v. *Kansas State University,* 861 P.2d 768 (Kan. 1993).

Peterson v. *San Francisco Community College District,* 685 P.2d 1193 (Cal. 1984).

Tanja H. v. *Regents of the University of California,* 278 Cal. Rprtr. 918 (Cal. Ct. App. 1991).

RICHARD FOSSEY is associate professor of education law and policy at Louisiana State University.

MICHAEL CLAY SMITH is professor of criminal justice at the University of Southern Mississippi.

Vigilant institutional oversight can prevent or circumscribe infractions.

The Liability of Colleges and Universities for Fraud, Waste, and Abuse in Federally Funded Grants and Projects

Steven D. Gordon

The federal government's intensified campaign in recent years to curb fraud, waste, and abuse in connection with the expenditure of federal funds has now reached the nation's institutions of higher learning. This fateful development is illustrated by the following events which have occurred during the past few years.

In November 1988 Dr. Stephen Breuning was convicted of two felonies in federal court based upon false statements he had made in seeking the renewal of a federal research grant as a faculty member at the University of Pittsburgh. He was sentenced to 60 days of confinement in a halfway house and 250 hours of community service. In addition, he was ordered to pay back $11,352 in salary and to stay out of psychological research for at least five years (*U.S.* v. *Breuning*, 1988). The University of Pittsburgh was not prosecuted (although, as will be discussed below, it could have been), but did reimburse the National Institute of Mental Health more than $163,000, representing grant money that went to the university to pay for Breuning's research.

In 1988 and 1989 the U.S. House of Representatives Committee on Government Operations held three separate hearings on the subject of scientific misconduct and conflicts of interest among researchers in the academic community.

This chapter originally appeared in *West's Education Law Reporter* and is reprinted by permission of West Publishing Company. Some footnotes have been deleted. Readers may consult the original article in *West's Education Law Reporter 75*, 13–28 (Aug. 13, 1992).

It investigated the Breuning episode and a number of other cases at universities across the country involving apparent scientific fraud or conflicts of interest. On September 10, 1990, the Committee issued a lengthy report discussing the nature and scope of the problem, and making certain findings and recommendations. One notable recommendation was as follows: "the committee believes that strong penalties should be levied on grantees who provide misleading information regarding research results or funding sources. These should include a mandatory 'debarring' from future grants for specified periods and mandatory reimbursement by both the institution and the investigator" [H.R. Rep. No. 688, 101st Cong., 2d Sess. 12 (1990), p. 68].

Most recently, a federal audit of Stanford University disclosed hundreds of thousands of dollars in questionable or unallowable charges billed to the government for federal research conducted on campus. Stanford responded by withdrawing or reversing many of these charges. A number of other leading colleges and universities have since followed suit. Harvard, MIT, Cornell, and Dartmouth are among the schools which, in the wake of the revelations regarding Stanford, have now returned or withdrawn overhead charges in the tens or hundreds of thousands of dollars (*Washington Post,* May 6, 1991, p. A13).

Although colleges and universities are not yet equated to defense contractors and other government contractors, they are no longer viewed as a breed apart. According to the president of the Association of American Universities, Robert Rosenzweig, "Universities have lost their immunity from public criticism. There's no longer a presumption in favor of their virtue" (*Washington Post,* May 6, 1991, p. A13).

Colleges and universities are tempting targets for government scrutiny, both because they have escaped it in the past and because they receive large amounts of federal funds. The General Accounting Office has estimated that colleges and universities will receive $9.2 billion in federal research funds [in 1992]. Federal agencies have become very aggressive in searching out instances of suspected fraud on the government and referring such matters for further investigation and possible sanctions. Government auditors frequently are urged to "think fraud" whenever they conduct an audit. Accordingly, colleges and universities have become—and will remain—vulnerable to incurring liability for fraud, waste, and abuse in the expenditure of public funds.

The potential liability of colleges and universities with respect to issues of fraud, waste, and abuse extends across three separate fronts—criminal, civil, and administrative. On the criminal front, federal prosecutors have made fraud upon the government a top priority and are prosecuting alleged offenders under several sweeping criminal statutes. Furthermore, the government has available a separate arsenal of civil and administrative sanctions to impose upon errant government contractors and program participants, either as an alternative to criminal prosecution or in addition thereto. This second arsenal has been significantly enhanced by Congress in recent years, and civil false claims suits were recently described by a top Justice Department official as "the government's primary weapon for fighting fraud"(*Corporate Crime Reporter,* Vol. 4,

No. 35, September 17, 1990, pp. 10–11). There is no question that this array of criminal, civil, and administrative sanctions will be utilized against some colleges and universities and/or their employees in the course of the next few years based on instances of alleged fraud, waste, and abuse of federal funds.

The purpose of this chapter is to review legal and practical aspects of a university's potential liability for fraud, waste, and abuse, and to discuss the array of criminal, civil, and administrative sanctions of which it must be aware.

Criminal Liability for Fraud

Criminal prosecutions of corporations have become increasingly popular with the federal government as a method of regulating institutional behavior. Such prosecutions are relatively low in cost and high in visibility and impact. Moreover, they usually are easy to win. As will be discussed below, corporations generally can be held criminally liable for the wrongdoing of an employee, notwithstanding that the corporation did not direct or encourage the misconduct. Colleges and universities are not exempt from such liability by reason of their non-profit status or public service mission. Although they may be less likely to be targeted for criminal prosecution than their for-profit counterparts, this is purely a matter of prosecutorial discretion.

It is well established that a corporation or an institution may be held criminally liable for violations committed by its employees, including lower level employees, if those employees (1) were acting within the scope of their authority, or apparent authority; and (2) were acting, at least in part, with intent to benefit the institution. An institution is not liable for an employee's criminal acts which were undertaken solely to advance the employee's own interests or those of a third party. Nonetheless, the institution is liable where its employee acted both for his own benefit *and* for the benefit of the employer (*United States v. Automated Medical Laboratories, Inc.*, 1985; *United States v. Gold*, 1985).

Moreover, as a general rule, a corporation may be held liable for the criminal violations of its employees committed within the scope of their authority even though such acts were contrary to corporate policy or express instructions by corporate management to the employees. However, although the mere existence of corporate or institutional policies and instructions prohibiting the conduct at issue does not provide a *legal* defense to criminal liability, a corporation may have a *factual* defense to liability in some instances if it can persuade the jury that it was sufficiently diligent in enforcing such policies or instructions.

The principal criminal statutes that prosecutors utilize to prosecute individuals or corporate entities for fraud in connection with the expenditure of federal funds are as follows.

False Statements. The criminal False Statements statute (18 U.S.C. § 1001) is the workhorse provision most often utilized by prosecutors in cases involving alleged fraud on the government. This statute is very broad in its reach. It prohibits both oral and written false statements, and any schemes to conceal or cover up material facts "in any matter within the jurisdiction of any . . . agency of the United States." Violation of this statute is a felony carrying a maximum penalty of five years' imprisonment.

There is no requirement that the statement in issue have been certified or made under oath (*United States* v. *Massey,* 1977). Further, the statement need not be made directly to a federal department or agency; the statute also covers any deception of an intermediary, for instance, a university (public or private) or a state or local agency, if that deception affects a federal agency. Thus, false statements may be within the reach of the statute even though the federal agency does not directly administer or fund a particular project or grant.

Likewise, the government does not have to show that it or anyone else actually relied on the alleged false statement. A statement may be "material" within the meaning of the False Statements statute even if it is ignored or never read by the party who received it. The statement simply must have been capable of influencing a decision by a federal agency relating to the performance of its functions (*Hughes* v. *United States,* 1990; *United States* v. *Swaim,* 1985). In that regard, false statements made to conceal a fraud are no less "material" than false statements designed to induce a fraud (*United States* v. *Brack,* 1984).

The statement in issue must be intentional and known to be false. However, virtually any sort of representation can be a criminal false statement that is *deliberately* dishonest. Indeed, even representations that are literally true can constitute false statements if, taken in context, they were deceptive and misleading. Moreover, in order to prove a defendant's guilty knowledge of a statement's falsity, it is not always necessary to demonstrate that he actually knew that the representation was false. Guilty knowledge can also be established by showing the defendant's reckless disregard for the truth or falsity of the statement, coupled with a conscious effort to avoid learning the truth (that is, deliberate ignorance or willful blindness).

Almost any sort of fraud or dishonesty can be prosecuted under the False Statements provision. Even conduct that does not inherently involve false representations often can be prosecuted under the False Statements statute because it violates some certification that the defendant is required to make. For example, there is no criminal statute which directly prohibits conflicts of interest by recipients of federal research grants, and many federal agencies have no restrictions on conflicts of interest for grantees. However, some agencies, such as the National Institute of Health (NIH), require grantees to list all sources of funding for research projects when they apply for NIH funds. Thus, the concealment of a conflict of interest by omitting a funding source on a grant application could give rise to a false statements prosecution.

The government typically requires certifications to be made regarding compliance with applicable laws or about matters which it considers especially important. Accordingly, universities and individual grant recipients should treat any certification requirements as "red flags" and take extra care to ensure that they are accurate since an erroneous certification may be viewed by the government as tantamount to prima facie evidence of a criminal false statement.

False Claims. The criminal False Claims statute (18 U.S.C. § 287) prohibits the knowing submission of a false, fictitious, or fraudulent claim to any agency of the United States. Violation of this provision is also a felony and carries a penalty of up to five years' imprisonment.

This sweeping prohibition is closely akin to the False Statements provision. While the definition of a "false claim" is considerably narrower than the all-encompassing definition of a "false statement," it is still quite broad. Any attempt to cause the government to part with its money constitutes a "claim" within the meaning of the provision. Furthermore, false statements made to forestall the government from recouping overpayments have also been held to violate the false claims prohibition (*United States* v. *Jackson*, 1988).

Each false demand for payment constitutes a separate violation of the statute, even if multiple claims are made pursuant to a single contract or grant, or are part of a single scheme to defraud. In addition, courts have held that otherwise valid claims for work performed under a federal contract or grant are transformed into criminal false claims if the contract or grant was procured by fraud in the first instance.

As in the case of false statements, the false claim need not have been submitted directly to the government; a defendant is culpable if he submits a claim to a private intermediary, such as a university, knowing that it will ultimately be passed on to the government or reimbursed by the government. While the claim must be submitted to the government, either directly or indirectly, there is no requirement that the claim actually be honored by the government (*United States* v. *Coachman*, 1984).

The guilty knowledge requirement of the false claims offense is essentially identical to that in the false statements provision, and can be satisfied in the same manner. Accordingly, guilty knowledge can be inferred from a defendant's reckless disregard for the truth or falsity of the claim, combined with a conscious effort to avoid learning the truth.

Conspiracy. If more than one person participated in perpetrating or attempting to perpetrate a fraud, then a conspiracy charge may be pursued by the government. The federal conspiracy statute defines two distinct conspiracy offenses: (1) conspiracy to violate some other federal criminal law, and (2) conspiracy to defraud the United States (18 U.S.C. § 371).

The first offense—conspiracy to violate some other criminal law—is significant for several reasons. First, it permits the government to prosecute an incomplete or unsuccessful attempt to commit some other offense, even if that other offense could not itself be charged because one or more essential elements are missing. The essence of the crime of conspiracy is an agreement to engage in a criminal act, and the successful completion of the act is not required. A defendant, therefore, can be convicted of conspiracy even if acquitted of the substantive offense. Second, a conspiracy charge provides an additional basis for criminal liability. A defendant can be convicted and sentenced for both the substantive offense and conspiracy to commit it. Third, a conspiracy makes any one defendant vicariously liable for the acts of all co-conspirators which are committed in furtherance of the conspiracy.

The second offense—conspiracy to defraud the United States—is potentially even more significant in the context of alleged frauds against the government. The concept of defrauding the United States has become so elastic over the years that it can potentially encompass any conduct which a court views as "collusive and dishonest" if some federal rule or regulation was violated in the process. The conspirators need not have intended to cause the government economic loss or a deprivation of property interests. The conspirators must "merely have agreed to interfere with or obstruct one of the government's lawful functions," whether or not the improper acts or objectives are themselves criminal under another statute (*United States* v. *Nersesian,* 1987; *United States* v. *Tuohey,* 1989). The "lawful functions" which are interfered with or obstructed can be established by "custom, practices, and regulations" of a federal agency. There is no requirement that a knowing violation of an agency's regulation take place, only that the conduct was collusive and dishonest, and that the conspirators' actions violated a duty reasonably owed to the government.

To establish the offense of conspiracy, the government must prove that (1) two or more persons entered into an unlawful agreement; (2) that the defendant knowingly became a member of the conspiracy; and (3) that at least one of the members of the conspiracy knowingly committed at least one act to further the objective of the conspiracy.

Where the participants in a conspiracy are all employees of the same institution, the question arises whether the institution itself can also be prosecuted for conspiracy. It has been argued that since the acts of corporate employees constitute acts of the corporation, and since a corporation cannot conspire with itself, it cannot conspire with its employees. However, this argument apparently has been rejected by all of the federal courts that have considered it. Those courts have uniformly held that a corporation can be convicted of criminal conspiracy for the acts of two or more of its agents conspiring together on behalf of the corporation. In contrast, a corporate employee, acting *alone* on behalf of the corporation, cannot be convicted of conspiring with the corporation.

Penalties Imposed Upon Conviction. The sentences imposed upon individual defendants in federal criminal cases are now governed by the new Federal Sentencing Guidelines. It is the announced intention of the Guidelines to increase the instances in which mandatory prison sentences are imposed for economic crimes.

Corporations convicted of a criminal offense obviously cannot be incarcerated, but are subject to significant fines in the event of conviction. The maximum fine that can be imposed upon organizational defendants is normally $500,000 or twice the pecuniary gain or loss resulting from the offense, whichever is greater (18 U.S.C. § 3571).

Civil Liability for Fraud

Attention must be paid to the distinct provisions that create civil liability for fraud upon the government. The magnitude of such civil liability often may be so significant as to be of nearly equal, and sometimes greater, concern than the applicable criminal penalties. Moreover, there is a substantially greater danger of being subjected to a civil fraud suit than a criminal prosecution. The government often is willing to pursue a civil false claims suit although it would decline criminal prosecution either because of the higher criminal burden of proof or as a matter of prosecutorial discretion. Indeed, as noted above, the Justice Department recently stated that the civil False Claims Act has become the government's primary weapon for fighting fraud. Finally, as will be discussed below, a criminal prosecution can only be instituted by the government, whereas civil false claim suits can be instituted and even prosecuted by private parties.

Civil False Claims Act. The civil False Claims Act (31 U.S.C. § 3729) imposes liability on anyone who knowingly presents a false or fraudulent claim to the government. Originally enacted after the Civil War, this provision was extensively amended in 1986 to expand its coverage and stiffen its penalties.

There are three elements that must be proven to establish liability in a basic false claims action: (1) presentation of the claim; (2) the falsity of the claim; and (3) the defendant's knowledge of the claim's falsity. The statute explicitly provides that the knowledge element can be satisfied by proof that the defendant had *actual knowledge* of the claim's falsity, or that he acted in *deliberate ignorance* of the truth or falsity of the claim, or that he acted in *reckless disregard* of the truth or falsity of the claim [31 U.S.C. § 3729(b)]. Proof of specific intent to defraud is not required, nor need it be shown that the government actually relied on the false claim.

The essential elements of an action under the False Claims Act normally will be identical to the elements of the criminal false claims offense. The 1986 amendments broadened the Act to include the making or use of a false statement to get a false claim paid, and conspiring to defraud the government by getting a false claim paid, thereby tracking the criminal statutes prohibiting false statements and conspiracies to defraud the government [31 U.S.C. § 3729(a)]. Thus, in some instances, the elements of a civil false claims action will parallel those other criminal offenses.

The fundamental distinction between a civil false claims action and the comparable criminal offense is the lower burden of proof needed to make out a civil action. Liability under the civil provision can be established by a preponderance of the evidence [31 U.S.C. § 3731(c)], while liability under the criminal provision must be proven beyond a reasonable doubt.

The congruence between a civil false claims action and the elements of a criminal prosecution has important implications. On one hand, the government often will be able to utilize a criminal conviction of a corporation or one of its employees to establish, without more, the corporation's liability under the civil False Claims Act. Conversely, the initiation of a civil false claims suit by a private party pursuant to the *qui tam* provision (discussed below) may well trigger a criminal fraud investigation by the government.

As in the realm of criminal liability, the rule of *respondeat superior* applies to civil false claims suits and makes a corporation liable for the wrongful acts of its employees committed within the scope of their employment (*United States v. Entin*, 1990). Indeed, in certain instances it may be possible to hold a corporation liable for an employee's fraud under the civil provision when no liability would attach under the criminal provision. As discussed above, a corporation is not criminally liable for employees' wrongful acts which were undertaken solely to advance the employees' own interests or those of a third party. However, there is a split in authority about whether a corporation can be held civilly liable under the False Claims Act in such circumstances.

It is more questionable whether a college or university can be held liable for false claims concerning grants which it administers and passes on to the government, but where the grantee who actually perpetrates the fraud is not a university employee. Absent a requirement that the university independently verify the accuracy of the information in the pertinent document, the university may not be liable unless it had knowledge of the fraud.

Apart from automatic liability imposed by the rule of *respondeat superior,* a college is also liable for submitting any claims which it "knew" to be false in some material respect. In civil false claims cases, the government is taking very aggressive positions about what quantum of evidence is sufficient to establish a defendant's "knowledge" of a claim's falsity. As discussed above, the statute explicitly provides that the knowledge requirement can be satisfied not only by proof of actual knowledge, but also by proof that the defendant acted in *deliberate ignorance* of a claim's falsity, or in *reckless disregard* of its truth or falsity.

The consequences of a shift to a gross negligence standard are significant. Not only is this a lower standard of proof, but it assesses culpability based on what the defendant *should have* known or done in the circumstances, without any consideration of the defendant's actual state of mind. Accordingly, it puts a premium on close compliance with any applicable standards of conduct for monitoring federal monies or grants. Such standards of conduct may be established by federal rules or regulations or even by the university's own practices in other areas. For example, one experienced government attorney has suggested that the requisite "reckless disregard" tantamount to knowledge of a false claim might be established by showing that a corporate defendant did not scrutinize claims passed on to the government for reimbursement as carefully as claims paid out of its own pocket.

Thus, the civil False Claims Act offers federal prosecutors the potent combination of stringent liability provisions and a relaxed burden of proof. At the same time, since it is styled as a purely civil or remedial action, there often is less reluctance to use this sanction than there would be to institute a criminal prosecution. It is little wonder then that civil false claims suits are increasingly the government's weapon of choice in responding to instances of perceived fraud, waste or abuse in the expenditure of federal funds.

Qui Tam Suits. There is another aspect to the civil False Claims Act that makes it even more menacing for federal contractors and grantees. A *qui tam* provision in the Act enables—and, indeed, encourages—this weapon to be unleashed by private litigants as well as federal prosecutors.

The 1986 amendments to the Act invigorated this *qui tam* provision, which theretofore had been seldom used (31 U.S.C. § 3730). The revised *qui tam* provision permits a private party to initiate a False Claims Act suit in the name of the Government. The suit is filed under seal with the court and the plaintiff must simultaneously serve the Government with a copy of the complaint and a written summary of his evidence. The Government is then given a period of 60 days (which can be extended upon its request) to study the case and decide whether to assume control of the suit. If the Government declines to take over the action, the plaintiff has the right to pursue it in the name of the Government. In either event, the suit is then unsealed by the court and the action proceeds [31 U.S.C. § 3730(b)].

The amended *qui tam* provision creates a substantial financial incentive for private parties to initiate and pursue False Claims Act suits by providing significant awards to those parties if the suit results in any recovery of money, either by trial or through settlement [31 U.S.C. § 3730(d)]. Significantly, the fact that the *qui tam* plaintiff may himself have "planned and initiated" the False Claims Act violation does not preclude him from receiving an award unless he has been criminally convicted for his role in the violation. Instead, the fact that the plaintiff was a participant in the violation simply gives the court the right to reduce his award to the extent it considers appropriate under all of the circumstances [31 U.S.C. § 3730(d)(3)].

Moreover, in addition to these financial incentives, the *qui tam* provision also provides "whistleblower" protection to any employee who is discharged, demoted, suspended, threatened, or harassed because of lawful acts done in furtherance of a *qui tam* action. These protected acts include investigation for, initiation of, testimony for, or assistance in a False Claims Act suit. The employee protections include reinstatement at the appropriate level of seniority, double back pay plus interest, any special damages, and reasonable attorneys' fees [31 U.S.C. § 3730(h)].

It requires little imagination to understand that the implications of the *qui tam* provision are enormous. In particular, disgruntled individuals are likely to seize upon the *qui tam* provision as a convenient means of retribution and potential enrichment.

In September 1990 the Assistant Attorney General in charge of the Justice Department's Civil Division stated that more than $70 million have been recovered through settling *qui tam* cases since the 1986 amendments to the False Claims Act and that $9 million of that total has gone to private plaintiffs.

Program Fraud Civil Remedies Act. This "mini-False Claims Act" (31 U.S.C. §§ 3806–3812), enacted in 1986, authorizes federal agencies to pursue by administrative adjudication smaller fraud cases that the Justice Department declines to litigate in court. There is a $150,000 ceiling on cases which may be brought under this law, calculated roughly on a per claim basis. Although this provision has been little used thus far, resort to it is likely to increase over the next few years.

The substantive provisions of this law are essentially the same as the civil False Claims Act. The government may recover an "assessment," of up to twice the amount of a false claim or portion of such claim which is false, and a civil penalty of not more than $5000 for each separate claim. This law is broader than the False Claims Act in one respect—it also provides for the imposition of a civil penalty of up to $5000 for false statements unrelated to a claim for payment if the statement is made in the context of an express certification or affirmation (31 U.S.C. § 3802). The agency must have Justice Department authorization before instituting an action under this law [31 U.S.C. § 3803(b)(2)].

Other Civil Remedies. There are several other civil remedies which the government can utilize in response to fraudulent practices by a contractor. The Contract Disputes Act (41 U.S.C. § 604) makes a contractor liable for any unsupported claim, or unsupported portion of a claim, even if the government did not pay it and suffered no loss. Furthermore, if a claim is tainted by fraud, then it is subject to forfeiture in its entirety (28 U.S.C. § 2514).

Administrative Sanctions: Suspension and Debarment

Apart from the arsenal of criminal and civil provisions discussed thus far, the government also has the ability to impose very significant administrative sanctions upon contractors and grantees who engage in fraudulent practices. In some situations, these sanctions may be the most important consequences of all because they enable the government to exclude an errant university or college from receiving any government contracts or grants.

There have long been provisions for the debarment and suspension of contractors with respect to federal *procurement* contracts. Suspension and debarment in this arena are governed by the Federal Acquisition Regulations. In the late 1980s, pursuant to Executive Order, the various federal departments and agencies established a corresponding government-wide system for *nonprocurement* debarment and suspension, thus embracing grantees and other recipients of federal funds.

Federal agencies have the authority to *debar* or exclude program participants who have engaged in misconduct from doing business with the federal government for a specified period of time. A participant which has been debarred by any federal agency is automatically excluded from participating in transactions throughout the executive branch of the federal government [34 C.F.R. §§ 85.100(a), 85.200(a)]. The length of the exclusion period is to be commensurate with the seriousness of the cause(s), generally not to exceed three years [34 C.F.R. § 85.320(a)].

The governing regulations list several different causes for debarment, including a catch-all provision (34 C.F.R. § 85.305). The most significant causes are: (1) a criminal conviction or civil judgment for fraud or comparable misconduct—including false statements and false claims—in obtaining or performing any public agreement or transaction; or (2) violation of the terms of a public agreement or transaction so serious as to justify debarment, such as a willful violation of a statutory or regulatory requirement.

In theory, debarment is not intended to be penal or punitive. Its stated purpose is to protect the government from unscrupulous or irresponsible program participants and to safeguard the integrity of government programs. Thus, the key issue in considering whether to debar a participant is supposed to be the *present responsibility* of the participant rather than its culpability for past conduct. In practice, however, federal agencies have often utilized debarment as an administrative sanction for past misconduct rather than as a prophylactic measure to protect against current or future misconduct. Debarment is an extraordinarily powerful sanction since it may cripple or destroy a participant in economic terms. In fact, the mere pendency of a debarment proceeding can have an adverse impact on the ability of a participant to conduct its normal business activities, and can significantly injure its reputation.

Moreover, a debarment action is considerably easier for the government to prosecute—and more difficult for a participant to defend against—than a civil or criminal suit. Since debarment is an administrative proceeding, there are far fewer procedural rights and protections afforded to a defendant than in a civil or criminal suit in federal court. The defendant is entitled to notice of the cause(s) being relied upon for debarment and an opportunity to submit a written response, but is not necessarily entitled to a hearing on the matter. Further, even if a hearing is granted, the defendant's rights to discovery, to compel the production of evidence and witnesses, and to cross-examine adverse witnesses are much more limited than they would be in a suit in federal court. The defendant can appeal an adverse decision to the federal courts but the scope of judicial review is limited.

Furthermore, a debarment is not necessarily linked to the particular individual that actually committed the misconduct in issue. Instead, the controlling regulations have sweeping provisions for attributing to related individuals and entities misconduct committed by one party and therefore extending the debarment to those related parties.

Under the provisions for imputing conduct, the misconduct of an employee, officer, or director may be imputed to a corporation when the misconduct occurred in connection with the individual's performance of duties on behalf of the corporation, or with the corporation's knowledge, approval, or acquiescence [34 C.F.R. § 85.325(b)(1)]. This, in essence, is the commonly applied rule of *respondeat superior.*

Beyond this rule, however, there are several additional provisions for imputing misconduct. First, there is a "reverse-*respondeat superior*" provision under which the misconduct of a corporation may be imputed to any employee, officer, or director who participated in, knew of, or had reason to know of the misconduct [34 C.F.R. § 85.325(b)(2)]. Second, there is a provision for imputing the misconduct of one participant to other participants in a joint venture. This provision permits the misconduct of one participant to be attributed to other participants if the misconduct occurred for or on behalf of the joint venture, or with the knowledge, approval, or acquiescence of the other participants. Moreover, the regulations provide that acceptance of the benefits derived from the misconduct shall be presumptive evidence of such knowledge, approval, or acquiescence [34 C.F.R. § 85.325(b)(3)]. Finally, the general provision on the scope of debarments provides that the debarment of an organization automatically includes all of its organizational elements unless the debarment decision is explicitly made more limited.

Conclusion

The federal government's war on fraud, waste, and abuse in the expenditure of federal funds has indeed reached academia. Those colleges and universities that fail to heed this development will leave themselves vulnerable to incurring harsh sanctions in the coming years.

As the Stanford incident and its fallout have demonstrated, many colleges and universities must tighten their accounting practices with regard to their own expenditures of, and billing for, federal funds. In addition, colleges and universities must recognize that they can incur liability for fraudulent practices perpetrated by their faculties and students with respect to federally funded projects, regardless of whether the institution itself is a party to the funding arrangement or a direct beneficiary thereof. The danger of such vicarious liability is greatest in those situations where the institution fails to respond adequately to allegations of misconduct that are brought to its attention, or else lacks basic oversight mechanisms that any responsible institution should have. This highlights the importance of internal investigations and procedural reviews as management and loss prevention tools.

Legal References

Hughes v. United States, 899 F.2d 1495 (6th Cir. 1990).
United States v. Automated Medical Laboratories, Inc., 770 F.2d 399 (4th Cir. 1985).
United States v. Brack, 747 F.2d 1142 (7th Cir. 1984), cert. denied, 469 U.S. 1216(1985).
United States v. Stephen E. Breuning, No. K-88–0135 (D. Md).
United States v. Coachman, 727 F.2d 1293(D.C.Cir. 1984).
United States v. Entin, 750 F.Supp. 512 (S.D.Fla. 1990).
United States v. Gold, 743 F.2d 800, 823 (11th Cir. 1984), cert. denied, 469 U.S. 1217 (1985).
United States v. Jackson, 845 F.2d 880 (9th Cir.), cert. denied, 488 U.S. 857(1988).
United States v. Massey, 550 F.2d 300 (5th Cir. 1977).
United States v. Nersesian, 824 F.2d 1294, 1313 (2d Cir.), cert. denied, 484 U.S. 957, 108 S.Ct. 355, 98 L.Ed.2d 380 (1987).
United States v. Swaim, 757 F.2d 1530 (5th Cir.), cert. denied, 474 U.S. 825 (1985).
United States v. Tuohey, 867 F.2d 534 (9th Cir. 1989).

Steven D. Gordon is an attorney in the Washington, D.C., law firm of Holland and Knight.

The admitted student with a criminal past poses special dilemmas.

Rescinding Offers of Admissions When Prior Criminality Is Revealed

Jerome W. D. Stokes, Allen W. Groves

Few high school students reach the heights achieved by Gina Grant in the winter of 1994–95. Ms. Grant had in hand an offer of early admission to Harvard in December 1994 followed by a glowing profile in the April 2, 1995, Sunday *Boston Globe,* highlighting her as a shining example of success triumphing over personal adversity. The article failed to mention Gina's single flaw: she had bludgeoned her mother to death in South Carolina in 1990. When this news surfaced, Harvard was severe: the admissions office withdrew its offer the following day.

Richie Parker, like Gina Grant, was, in the winter of 1994–95, at the peak of high school student success. Rated as a high school basketball All-American, and one of the top twenty-five high school basketball players in the nation, the 6'5" Parker received scholarship offers to play basketball at Seton Hall University, George Washington University, and the University of Utah. Seton Hall topped his list, having offered him a full four-year athletic scholarship, contingent upon only one circumstance: Parker must avoid a prison term.

Like Gina Grant, Parker, too, had a problem of criminality in his past. In January 1994, when he was seventeen, Parker and a friend sexually assaulted a fifteen-year-old girl they cornered in a stairwell at Manhattan Central High School. After plea-bargaining for five years' probation, Parker was free to accept

This article originally appeared in *West's Education Law Reporter* and is reprinted by permission of West Publishing Company. Some footnotes have been deleted. Readers may consult the original article in *West's Education Law Reporter 105,* 76–85 (Feb. 22, 1996).

55

Seton Hall's offer. Two months later, however, a public firestorm broke over his scholarship offer. Within days, chancellor Thomas Peterson announced the withdrawal of Parker's athletic grant-in-aid.

While news of Grant's fate prompted calls for a "second chance" and paeans on the value of redemption, Parker's reversal resulted in equally strong public denouncement of an endorsement of those same ideals.

Since Grant is white and Parker is black, some have seen these contrasting public reactions as further evidence of the racial double standard in American life. Others believe the reactions expose our antipodal views on the relative risks that males and females pose of repeat offense. The fundamental and more significant question each case poses, however, is the same: When a college or university applicant arrives carrying the baggage of a past crime of violence, is there room in the Big House with all its marvelous—but oblivious—occupants? What standards should guide admissions officers seeking to weigh the virtues of redemption against the risk of recidivism?

The solution depends in large part upon the answer to a host of related questions. For example, what is the mission of colleges and universities, and where do such cases fit into that mission? To whom is the greater duty owed: the applicant seeking an opportunity for redemption and rehabilitation, if not, in Ms. Grant's case, reinvention? Or the university community into whose innocent midst the once-violent student will be admitted? Is it possible to strike a balance between these competing and conflicting duties? What are the public policy implications of such a choice, and what potential liabilities are involved?

Underlying the public debate concerning the Grant and Parker cases is a relatively straightforward concern: Who should be called to answer if an admissions officer makes the "wrong" decision and a once-violent applicant enrolled as a student turns violent again, with grave consequences to others in the university community? This chapter seeks to explore the answers to these questions, using the Grant and Parker cases to illustrate both the need for clear legal standards to guide the decision-making process and the difficulty in attempting to presage such guidelines.

Gina Grant

Because Gina Grant was a juvenile at the time she murdered her mother, records of Grant's plea and sentence were, pursuant to statute, sealed. But Grant's sensational case received extensive press coverage in South Carolina thus becoming a matter of public record. It was also a matter of much public discourse, infused with a certain amount of sympathy for the fourteen-year-old defendant. At the time many argued that Grant's actions were justified—that she had acted in self-defense. Personal affirmations of the girl's character were plenty citing an otherwise exemplary life.

The cards that Gina Grant were dealt in life were anything but winning. Gina's father died of cancer when she was eleven, and her mother was, so several witnesses testified, an abusive alcoholic who was known to clash frequently with her daughter. No evidence of any actual physical abuse, however, was ever submitted.

In contrast, the county prosecutor pointed to evidence showing Grant's efforts to conceal the murder, first by stabbing a knife into her mother's neck, claiming her death a suicide, and then later by attempting to blame her mother's death on her own boyfriend, whose help she had solicited in the initial cover-up effort. None of these acts reflected traits likely to impress a choosey admissions office.

Grant ultimately pleaded no contest in juvenile court to charges of voluntary manslaughter. She was sentenced to serve a mere six months in detention, with probation to follow until age eighteen. After serving her detention, Grant petitioned for permission to leave South Carolina and move to Massachusetts so that she could serve out her probation with an aunt and uncle. Grant's request was granted, despite the strong opposition of the South Carolina parole board, which deemed her crime singularly detestable. The board wanted Grant to remain incarcerated until she was able to recall specific events of the night her mother was killed and would accept responsibility for her actions.

Not long after arriving in Massachusetts, at age sixteen Grant moved out on her own, relying for financial support on a trust established after her father's death, as well as on a portion of her mother's estate. Grant enrolled in the highly respected Cambridge Rindge and Latin High School, where she achieved academic success, served as captain of the tennis team, and worked with underprivileged youth in the local community.

Applying to Harvard as part of its early decision program for exceptional candidates, Grant received an offer of admission. She had not been entirely forthcoming about her role in her mother's death four years earlier. In fact, she lied, telling a Harvard interviewer that her mother had died in an automobile accident (*Boston Herald,* May 11, 1995, p. 1). Her seemingly remarkable triumph over personal losses drew the attention of the *Boston Globe,* which featured Grant in an article celebrating her academic success despite being orphaned years before. When the *Globe* reporter asked about the circumstances of her mother's death, Grant demurred. It was, she said guardedly, "too painful to discuss" (*Boston Globe,* April 7, 1995, p. 1).

Others were not so withholding. As Grant basked in the media spotlight, copies of newspaper clippings from Grant's South Carolina pleas and sentence proceedings were being anonymously mailed to both Harvard and the *Boston Globe.* Stunned by the revelation, on April 3, 1995, Harvard withdrew its offer of admission, claiming that Grant had been dishonest in her application by failing to indicate her prior probation imposed by the South Carolina court. Harvard students, joined by numerous public commentators, rose in protest. All criticized the university for failing to recognize Grant as a model of the juvenile justice system and as a testament to the value of redemption.

On June 6, 1995, Grant graduated with honors from Cambridge Rindge and Latin, and was one of five students chosen for the Estelle Paris Scholarship, awarded by Cambridge Hospital. Denied admission to Harvard and, subsequently, to Columbia University as well, Grant accepted a place in the freshman class at Tufts, where she enrolled on August 30, 1995. Whereas Harvard's student body expressed admiration and support for their would-be alumna, students at Tufts reacted with alarm. Awaiting Grant's arrival were hundreds of fliers posted and distributed by a conservative student newspaper accusing the Tufts administration of admitting a "killer" to the school.

Richie Parker

In January 1995, as Richie Parker began the final semester of his senior year, his criminal case went to trial. The trial judge would later aver that prosecutors had sufficient evidence to convict Parker of first-degree sodomy, punishable by a maximum jail term of twenty-four years. The state, however, accepted Parker's plea bargain of felony sex abuse instead.

Unlike Gina Grant, Richie Parker never denied his role in the violent act of January 1994. In fact, he went so far as to publicly apologize to his victim, offering to pay her a percentage of his future income as a professional basketball player to settle a civil action brought against him.

Resolution of Parker's criminal charges left him free to pursue basketball at Seton Hall University. Then, a *New York Post* article challenged Seton Hall Chancellor Thomas Peterson, a Catholic priest, to explain to the fathers of Seton Hall's female students "why the school is so eager to allow an academically unsound sex felon to freely walk . . . in their daughters' company" (*U.S. News & World Report,* July 17, 1995, p. 18). Three days after the article appeared, Seton Hall withdrew its offer. Parker, Chancellor Peterson allowed, "should be given a second chance, but not here . . . I didn't want to send the wrong message to the thousands of women we have here."

Released by Seton Hall, Parker accepted a scholarship offer from George Washington University, whose head basketball coach, Mike Jarvis, felt Parker deserved a chance for redemption. Just as with Seton Hall, GWU soon found itself defending its decision before its shocked and outraged students. Faculty and alumni eyed Parker's future enrollment with distaste and embarrassment. Attempting to stem this angry tide, GWU amiably offered a full scholarship to Parker's victim, while Parker's attorney, his pastor, his family, his coach, his friends, and even his victim went public, urging a second chance for the basketball star. The outcry, however, did not subside, and GWU withdrew Parker's scholarship offer on June 29, 1995.

Fleeing west, Parker sought out Mesa Community College coach Rob Standifer and asked for a chance to play basketball in Arizona. Standifer offered Parker a place on the team, but failed to inform his superiors about his star recruit's criminal past until two days before Parker was to arrive on campus. The media maelstrom followed Parker to Mesa, where the reaction was summary. Coach Standifer was forced to resign, and Parker was told that although he could remain at the school, he would not be permitted to play on the basketball team. Parker remains at Mesa, hoping to transfer to a top college program next year after the memory of his crime fades.

The Duty of Reasonable Care Owed to Business Invitees

Unfortunately student injuries from third-party assaults are not uncommon on the modern college campus. Courts are frequently asked to determine whether the college itself may be called to answer for those injuries. Few are willing to require colleges to be absolute guarantors against every injury or assault on their students by others. Today, adult college students are generally deemed to share significant responsibility for their own safety and security. This rejection of the doctrine of in loco parentis in the college setting has led courts to refuse to impose a heightened, "special duty" based solely upon an injured plaintiff's status as a student enrolled in the institution.

Courts have been willing to hold colleges to the same standard of care applied to businesses who invite the public onto their premises. A person is considered a "business invitee" on the property of another if (1) the person enters by express or implied invitation; (2) the entry is connected with the owner's business or with an activity conducted by the owner on the land; and (3) the owner receives a benefit (see, for example, *Leonardi* v. *Bradley University*, 1993). The duty owed to a business invitee, the highest level of duty owed by a property owner, is that of "reasonable care for the invitee's personal safety . . . with respect to conditions on the premises which pose an unreasonable risk of harm. This duty includes a responsibility to ascertain, as well as warn of, dangerous conditions" (*Leonardi* v. *Bradley University*, 1993).

Not surprisingly, the majority of reported cases involve conditions or defects on the premises such as poor lighting in a stairwell (*Tanja H.* v. *Regents of the University of California*, 1991), overgrown foliage (*Peterson* v. *San Francisco Community College District*, 1984), or broken door locks (*Delaney* v. *University of Houston*, 1992) that are alleged to have contributed to, or otherwise made possible an assault on a third party. The analogy to business invitee claims in the general commercial setting is thus clear, since the initial question remains the same: whether the business/college maintained its grounds or facilities negligently, thus breaching the duty of care owed to its invitees/students.

Simply demonstrating a defect in the creation or maintenance of a physical condition, however, is not enough to establish liability. The complaining student must also show a connection between the assault and that defective condition. This is generally achieved by showing that the assault was foreseeable to the university, and that the physical condition actually made possible, and thus proximately caused, the assault. In many cases, foreseeability is established by the presence of facts showing the college's knowledge of similar assaults in the same general area in which the plaintiff was assaulted and injured.

But what about a claim that the admission of a student with a known prior propensity for violence was itself the negligent act that caused the assault and resulting injury? Can a fellow student be a "dangerous condition" as described in the business invitee cases described above? In the view of several courts, the answer is yes, where it can be established that the university had knowledge of prior similar assaults by the particular actor and failed to take appropriate action.

In theory, this question of foreseeability based upon prior conduct may not be difficult to apply. But in practice, an institution faces a curious problem: Which details of an applicant's crime and punishment should be taken into account? Consider two hypothetical scenarios. First, assume that in her sophomore year at Tufts, Gina Grant attempts to stab her roommate during an argument. Second, assume that in his sophomore year at Mesa Community College, Richie Parker sexually assaults a female student late one evening in his co-educational dormitory.[1] Should either hypothetical second assault be deemed to have been foreseeable at the time the original admissions decision was made? Perhaps a stronger case for foreseeability can be made in Parker's case, since in the hypothetical presented, the post-admission activity—a sexual assault against a fellow student—is the same act as that committed prior to, and known at the time of, the admissions decision. Significant, too, might be the fact that Parker's prior assault occurred less than two years prior to admission, and thus is relatively close in proximity to the [hypothetical] repeat offense. By contrast, Grant's [hypothetical] assault might be less foreseeable, for the same reasons. Grant's prior act—killing an allegedly abusive, alcoholic parent—is arguably situation-based and thus less apt to be repeated, and further, was committed almost five years prior to her college enrollment.

Yet what if one also considers additional factors, such as Parker's acknowledgment of and apology for his prior crime, in contrast to Grant's apparent failure to express remorse and her attempted cover-up of her true involvement in her mother's death—which continued through the time of her efforts to gain college admission five years thereafter? Do these additional factors tip the foreseeability balance to one side or the other in either case? At the very least, they demonstrate the great difficulty in most cases of determining what is truly foreseeable and what is not.

This brings our inquiry back to the search for a meaningful standard by which to guide and review a university's decision to admit an applicant with a prior act of violence in his or her past. Although the "business invitee" cases concerning premises liability offer some insight, they may not provide an adequately clear and detailed standard. There may be other areas of commercial law that may be more closely akin to the college admissions process.

Toward a Theory of Negligent Admission

Courts have generally been willing to find a duty of care arising out of the performance of certain functions by the university, such as campus security, reasoning that once the school elects to undertake such functions, it must do so within a certain standard of care. (See, for example, *Mullins* v. *Pine Manor College,* 1983.) Does a similar standard of care apply to the university's conduct in carrying out its admissions decisions? If the duty to exercise reasonable care does extend to the admissions process, what level of investigation, evaluation, or decision making is required to satisfy that duty when considering an applicant with a violent past? Does the university's obligation end with consideration of the four corners of the application submitted by the prospective student? Is there an additional obligation to notify or "warn" the general community of the new student's violent past? Should admissions officers conduct an investigation beyond the information disclosed on the application form?

Consider the rapidly developing area of employment law known as "negligent hiring." In a negligent hiring claim, "the issue of liability primarily focuses on the adequacy of the employer's pre-employment investigation into the employee's background" (*Garcia* v. *Duffy,* 1986, p. 438). Under this legal theory, an employer may be found liable for injuries to a co-employee or business invitee inflicted by another employee where it is established that: (1) the employer knew or, in the exercise of ordinary care, should have known of its employee's propensity for violence or other unfitness at the time of hiring; (2) the employer nevertheless hired the employee; and (3) the negligently hired employee proximately caused the resulting injuries to plaintiff. (See, for example, *Carlsen* v. *Wackenhut Corporation,* 1994; *Plains Resources, Inc.* v. *Gable,* 1984; and *Garcia* v. *Duffy,* 1986.)

At least one legal commentator has suggested that negligent hiring standards should be applied to claims of negligence in the university admissions process, noting that

> these theories . . . appear to be at least as applicable to university students as they do to employees. When a university admits a student, it puts that student into intimate contact with other students. Some students see each other all day, every day, and share eating and living quarters as well. Further, university students live in a competitive, high-pressure environment that produces considerable stress, and it is not unreasonable to conclude that this stress might lead some individuals to commit acts of violence. If a student is prone to this kind of violent behavior, the university is therefore putting other students at risk. Thus, one can make the following argument: If a student commits a violent act against another student, and the university could have avoided the incident, the theory of "negligent admitting" could apply to the university, making it responsible for any injury that results. The university could avoid liability by asking appropriate questions of student applicants and acting reasonably upon the answers—in some cases, excluding students who are prone to violent behavior. [*Chicago Daily Law Bulletin,* 1995, p. 6]

Under this "negligent admitting" standard, a full-scale investigation would not necessarily be required in all instances. In most cases, a simple review of the application materials and follow-up interview, if available, would be sufficient. As in the negligent hiring context, a balancing test would be employed to determine if a given applicant appeared to require the extra burden of a more thorough background check, which would include the nature of the prior crime, the risk posed to other students by admitting the applicant, and any measures that might be taken to reduce the risk involved.

The standard of care imposed under a cause of action for negligent admitting would require that an additional inquiry be made in two distinct classes of cases. The first group would include those in which a careful review of the application materials identified "red flags" that would lead a reasonable person to conclude that some risk of harm might be posed by admitting a specific applicant. Such "red flags" might include an otherwise unusual absence of information provided by the applicant, as well as "inconsistencies on the face of his applications" (*Carlsen v. Wackenhut Corporation,* 1994, p. 886). The second class of cases would include those in which an applicant discloses prior criminal or violent activity, which again would cause a reasonable person to conclude that a risk of harm may exist. In both types of cases, an additional inquiry would be required, with the specific parameters of that inquiry established by the facts of the case and the information revealed thereunder. Even with special circumstances, however, there would be no legal requirement that the admissions officer make an inquiry with law enforcement agencies about an applicant's possible criminal record.

One difficulty in determining the scope of the admissions officer's duty in this regard is the lack of information available from which to make an assessment of risk, which may be further complicated by concerns regarding the veracity of the applicant providing that limited information. Consider Gina Grant's case. Harvard's stated basis for withdrawing Grant's offer of admission was not Grant's prior crime, but rather, Harvard's contention that Grant lied on her application by failing to acknowledge her prior probation as a result of that crime. Yet Harvard's application form does not inquire into prior convictions as a juvenile, and under Massachusetts law, Grant was under no obligation to include such information. Indeed, in her defense, Grant claimed that she had failed to mention her manslaughter plea and subsequent detention and probation precisely because she believed it was a sealed record and beyond inquiry. Moreover, an honest person could read the specific portion of the Harvard application—which asks whether "in the last three years you have incurred serious or repeated disciplinary action or if you have been dismissed, suspended or separated from school" or placed on probation—as seeking only instances of academic-related disciplinary action, since it does not explicitly inquire into criminal convictions, related probation or even "prior bad acts" as referred to in the Federal Rules of Evidence.

Like the Harvard paperwork, the George Washington application form that Richie Parker would have submitted fails to ask applicants whether they have a prior criminal conviction. In Parker's case, as in Grant's, a review of the basic application materials would have revealed nothing reflecting either applicant's violent acts. Unless an admissions officer happened to have been aware of the publicity that surrounded either case, he or she might never see fit to investigate either applicant further.

Yet this absence of available facts is by no means universal. For example, the application form utilized by the University of North Carolina–Chapel Hill specifically asks applicants whether they have "ever been convicted of a crime other than a minor traffic altercation" and whether they have "any charges pending at this time." If an applicant checks "yes" to these questions, the application is forwarded to a special committee, which examines the specific offense in question and holds a personal hearing with the applicant for further inquiry and explanation.

Assuming that the institution is located in a state that permits inquiry into prior criminal convictions, the UNC approach offers the best opportunity for gathering relevant information through identification of essential background facts and further inquiry, as well as affording some measure of due process to the applicant. Yet even under this approach, there remains the question of whether a university admissions officer or committee is really qualified to assess the gravity of prior violent conduct and the foreseeable risk of future such conduct under stressful circumstances.

"The problem," says Christoph Guttentag, director of admissions at Duke University, "is that every case is unique and different. Being arrested is different from being charged as a felon. Not all crimes are the same, and not all serious crimes are the same." Guttentag concedes that the Grant case "makes us think about some serious issues. At what point has a person paid his debt to society? And how does an institution balance the rights of an individual with the rights of the community?" (*Herald Sun* [Durham, NC], Apr. 23, 1995, p. G7)

Similarly, George Washington president Stephen Joel Trachtenberg, comparing his ultimate decision on Parker with Harvard's on Grant, has explained that "King Solomon had an easy time of it. . . . It's hard to resist the temptation to wonder if [Harvard] would have accepted [Grant] had she written . . . that she had beaten her mother to death with a candlestick. . . . It goes against the grain of GW . . . to write off any young person. . . . On the other hand, sexual crimes or crimes of violence are not the same as a shaky math SAT score or a proven inability to learn French" (*Washington Post,* July 16, 1995, p. F1).

The Grant and Parker cases illustrate the difficulty in balancing the hope of redemption and a productive future against the foreseeable risk of recidivism. For example, George Washington men's basketball coach Mike Jarvis, a Parker supporter, believes that universities "are here to take risks, educated risks. . . . Nobody should be judged on one act" (*Washington Post,* July 16, 1995, p. F1).

In evaluating whether to offer Parker a scholarship despite his sexual assault, Jarvis says he "looked at the other ninety-nine percent of his life" and determined that "the stairwell attack was an aberration." While Jarvis concedes that he has heard complaints from fathers concerned that their daughters might have to live in the same dormitory as Parker, he says that he asks them "to consider who's more dangerous, someone like the girl at Harvard [Sinedu Tadesse] who from out of nowhere killed her roommate, or someone whose problem we know" (*Washington Post,* July 16, 1995, p. F1).

Similarly, Harvard law professor Alan Dershowitz, commenting on Grant's situation, has offered his view that "it is unlikely that Ms. Grant poses any current danger, since intra-family murders carry a relatively low risk of recidivism" (*Buffalo News,* Apr. 21, 1995, p. V3). Boston University President John Silber concurs with this view, explaining that "students don't have any reason to fear her. There's no reason on earth to believe that [Grant] is going to kill anybody else. The conditions under which that death took place are very special, particular situations" (CNN, *Crossfire,* Aug. 31, 1995).

Others are not so sure. Stanton Samenow, for example. Samenow, an Alexandria, Virginia, forensic psychologist and author of *Inside the Criminal Mind,* has studied hundreds of young sex offenders over twenty-five years. Samenow disagrees with Mike Jarvis' opinion that Parker's sexual assault was an aberration in his life. "There is no such thing as an aberration," he says. "If an incident occurs of coercive sexual behavior, this is not an aberration. It makes a statement about a person. It is the tip of the iceberg" (*Washington Post,* July 16, 1995, p. F1). Similarly, a source in the Manhattan district attorney's office has reacted angrily to inquiries from college administrators seeking redemptive information on Richie Parker, reminding them of the nature of Parker's crime. The source then asks the administrators: "What more do you need to know?" (*Newsday* [N.Y.], Oct. 22, 1995, p. 37).

Consider as well the evaluation of those close to the case. Lexington County, South Carolina, Sheriff James Metts, who investigated Grant's crime in 1990, recently stated, "I'm not saying that she's a sociopath, but something about that girl concerns me. I think she's very cunning. I think she's manipulative" (*The Guardian,* Apr. 24, 1995, p. T4). And Lexington County prosecutor Donnie Myers agrees, stating that "[we] never, never had any question whatsoever about her mind. We had a tremendous question about her heart. Because I don't see where she showed any remorse whatsoever" (*Boston Herald,* Apr. 9, 1995, p. 7).

Even Alan Dershowitz has acknowledged that "the other part of Ms. Grant's crime—a deliberate attempt to cover up the killing—does . . . pose considerable risk of repetition" (*Buffalo News,* Apr. 21, 1995, p. V3).

The point of these divergent views is clear: if a noted law professor, a police officer, a forensic psychologist, and a basketball coach cannot agree on the degree of risk posed by an individual about whose case they have varying degrees of available facts and personal familiarity, how reasonable is it to expect an admissions officer or committee to make that same evaluation based upon a written application or brief interview? It is at least problematic to believe that an appropriate risk analysis can be conducted in a given case. To do so, we must trust an admissions committee to make an ad hoc evaluation of a given applicant's psychological makeup. Indeed, given that the American Psychiatric Association has acknowledged that "two out of three predictions of long-term future violence made by psychiatrists are *wrong*," (*Barefoot* v. *Estelle*, 1983, p. 920, [Blackmun, J., dissenting, emphasis supplied]), it may be dubious for a committee to try.

To further cloud the issue, there are differing views on whether our public policy goals should favor redemption and a clean start over the potential safety concerns of the general university community. Columnist Ellen Goodman's April 1995 editorial on the Grant case provides an excellent perspective on this dilemma.

> The debate from Harvard yard to "Nightline" has been about the rights of a juvenile offender and the behavior of the university—about unsealed records and second chances. . . . Most of us believe in rehabilitation, the idea that people, like houses, can be stripped down to the walls and rebuilt. But we also believe that the old structure may remain intact under the new wallpaper. . . . The people protesting Harvard's arrogance today might have had a lot to say about its ignorance tomorrow. Gina Grant was not, after all, convicted of shoplifting. She is guilty of murder. I have no idea what is in her mind or her nightmares. . . . Harvard was well within the boundaries of fairness when it acted on its doubt. [*Baltimore Sun,* Apr. 19, 1995, p. 21A]

Another commentator contends that Grant's risk of recidivism is "too unpredictable" to gauge; "she had already killed her mother, so what would she do the first time her roommate played the music too loud, or borrowed her leather jacket? There was no way to know" (*Herald-Sun* [Durham, NC], June 4, 1995, p. G7).

Of course, the answer is that we simply cannot know with any degree of certainty, and neither can an admissions officer, a basketball coach, a lawyer, or a forensic psychologist. So we return to our central questions: who should decide, and on what basis? If we accept that no one can really know what lies in Grant's or Parker's mind or nightmares, are we prepared to accept a bright-line rule under which no evaluation of redemption versus recidivism may be made by the college admissions decision maker?

The consequences of such a position are clear. If one believes that a university admissions committee is not qualified to assess the risk of recidivism in any case, then perhaps the prior act should not be considered at all. Under this view, the only proper decision makers as to redemption and the risk of recidivism are the judge and jury who hear the facts, determine guilt, and assess the penalty deemed appropriate, along with the parole committee or probation officer who determine when the individual is safe to return to society. The university cannot thereafter second-guess that decision, and after a sentence has been served, the prior crime becomes a nonissue in the admissions process. As a result, the university is effectively immunized from any legal claims should recidivism occur after enrollment, since a clear public policy has been imposed upon the admissions process requiring an initial assumption of redemption.

Support for this view may be found in *Eiseman* v. *State of New York* (1987), in which a convicted felon was released from prison, admitted to the State University College at Buffalo pursuant to a special program created by the legislature, and thereafter raped and murdered other students. In determining that the university was not liable for these crimes, the court noted that the assailant entered the university as part of a program that provided that admission was mandatory if the applicant satisfied certain criteria set by law, and thus there was no "heightened duty of inquiry" nor a duty to restrict access to other students or warn of his presence on campus. According to the court, strong public policy considerations supported this conclusion:

> His release and return to society . . . was mandated by law as well as by public policy, which have as their objectives rehabilitating and reintegrating former inmates in the hope that they will spend their future years productively instead of returning to crime. To this end, the value of education—both as an escape from society's underclass, and as a benefit to the public generally—is apparent. . . . But even more fundamentally, the underlying premise that, once released, Campbell by reason of his past preemptively posed a continuing foreseeable risk of harm to the community is at odds with the laws and public policy regarding the release of prisoners. Consistent with conditions of parole, an individual returned to freedom can frequent places of public accommodation, secure employment, and if qualified become a student. On any other theory, former inmates cannot be returned to society without imposing on those who open doors to them the risk of absolute liability for their acts. Nor did the college have a duty to restrict Campbell, as a student, even assuming it had a right to control his contacts with students. Publicly branding him on campus, as a former convict and former drug addict would have run up against the same laws and policies that prevented discriminating against him. . . . Imposing liability on the College for failing to screen out or detect potential danger signals in Campbell would hold the college to a higher duty than society's experts in making such predictions—the correction and parole officers, who in the present case have been found to have acted without negligence. [*Eiseman* v. *State of New York*, 1987, p. 1137]

The simplicity and apparent ease of application of a bright-line standard of "non-consideration" and default to the judicial system appeals to many, including Richie Parker, who when recently asked whether there is any limit to the magnitude of a mistake that is deserving of a second chance, responded that "a judge should make that decision" (*Washington Post*, July 16, 1995, p. F1). Other proponents include Tufts University, whose spokeswoman Rosemarie Van Camp has offered that "having paid her debts to society, [Grant] should not be denied the opportunity of pursuing a college degree" (*Charleston Gazette*, Aug. 21, 1995, p. 3A), and Boston University President John Silber, who recently stated that "a judge has heard [Grant's] case[,] she has been tried by the law [and] given six months in a correctional institution . . . and then put on probation. . . . Redemption has its place" (CNN, *Crossfire*, Aug. 31, 1995).

Yet there are many within both the educational and legal communities who would disagree with a bright-line, no-consideration and no-liability standard as too wooden, an abdication of the university's duty and mission, and a potentially unreasonable risk to others within the university that might leave them without compensation for any injuries inflicted by the hand of an insolvent perpetrator. If one is thus unwilling to shift to the courts or legislature the sole responsibility for weighing redemption versus recidivism in the college admissions process, then retaining such discretion by the university should bring with it a certain legal duty and its concomitant risk of liability.

What standard of care should frame this legal duty, or viewed differently, under what standard should a given admissions decision be made and later judged? Whatever standard is ultimately selected must provide some minimum factors to be considered by an admissions committee in weighing the particular crime, punishment, redemption, and risk of recidivism involved in a given case. These should include the nature of the crime, including the level of violence involved and any mitigating circumstances. Also significant is any meaningful evidence of rehabilitation since the crime, including remorse and acceptance of responsibility. Relevant, too, may be the amount of time that has passed since the crime was committed. In each decision, no small degree of subjectivity will exist, as will some degree of risk. Consider Mesa Community College spokesman David Irwin's acknowledgment that although several major college coaches remain eager to have Parker on their basketball court, "no one wants to be the first to touch him but a year from now, it will be a lot easier decision. If he can stay out of trouble, he's got a track record they can look at. A year from now, if he doesn't get in trouble, they can say, 'Maybe it was a youthful mistake'" (*Arizona Republic*, Aug. 30, 1995, p. D1).

Assuming that a decision is made to admit an applicant with a violent or criminal past, what steps must be taken to provide for the applicant's appropriate integration into the university community? For example, Gina Grant has been assigned to a single room in an upperclass dormitory at Tufts, rather than to a freshman dormitory with a roommate. Although Tufts isn't saying whether this decision was made as a result of Grant's past, would such an accommodation be enough? What could the university be expected to do in a given case?

Where the student's prior crime is known to the university admissions office but not the general community, should there be a duty to inform all or some of that community of that fact? As a general rule, absent a special relationship or power to control, there is no general legal duty to warn those who may be endangered by the conduct of another. Yet "what student wouldn't want to know if a convicted rapist was on her dormitory floor" (*Baltimore Sun*, Apr. 19, 1995, p. 21A). In this regard, consider *Nero* v. *Kansas State University* (1993), in which the court determined that a jury must decide such issues, and refused to release the university from liability as a matter of law. According to the court:

> Here, KSU knew of the alleged [prior] rape and had taken reasonable steps
> under the circumstances—i.e., it removed [assailant] from the coed dormitory

and moved him across campus and into an all-male dormitory. The university requested that [assailant] stay away from the coed dorm and the food service building. School was ending, and [assailant] was allowed to finish the semester. When [assailant] enrolled for intersession, KSU had the option of refusing to rent space to him. Instead, the university placed him in a coed dorm with the plaintiff [Nero], who is from a different state and presumably had no knowledge of the pending rape charge against [assailant]. Nero knew [assailant] was a fellow student living in the same dormitory, which may have given her a false sense of security. She ended up alone with [assailant] in a public area. Had [assailant] been a stranger and not living in the same dormitory, Nero might have been more likely to protect herself by immediately leaving the area. We are of the opinion reasonable people would disagree whether [assailant's] attack on Nero was foreseeable. [p. 780]

Consider also the view that "the acceptance of known murderers to campus life opens the debate about the purpose of rehabilitation and our core beliefs in the power of redemption. . . . Too often overlooked in the redemptive process, however, is the responsibility universities have to law-abiding students. These young people have a right to expect that the school will ensure their safety, or at least inform them of the fact that there is a murderer in their midst" (*Phoenix Gazette*, June 1, 1995, p. B8).

Does the primary goal of the juvenile and criminal justice system—rehabilitation and redemption—warrant a "clean slate" from references to past mistakes? Or does each member of the university community have a right to know these facts, and make its own individual decision whether to forgive and forget the past? While the few courts to have addressed this issue have come down in favor of privacy and redemption, the increasing public and legislative support for notification laws and victim's rights may yet turn the tide.

Consider the case of Barry Leavitt. Convicted of a brutal multiple-stabbing murder while a twenty-year-old college student in 1965, Leavitt was released from prison in 1974. Looking to turn his life around, Leavitt applied for admission to the University of Rhode Island. According to William Tirpaeck, URI's director of housing at the time, the school took a "gamble" and admitted Leavitt, housing him in a dormitory where few students knew of his past, and giving him a job in campus security which provided Leavitt access to every dormitory room on campus (*Providence Journal-Bulletin*, Apr. 22, 1995, p. A1). Leavitt ultimately graduated with a degree in engineering and accepted a job with General Electric, where, by 1992, he had advanced to the position of senior jet engine propulsion engineer. Clearly, Leavitt is a model of the redemptive process in higher education, and proved a good risk. But is there any doubt that the public outcry would have been great if Leavitt had harmed another student and evidence of URI's "gamble" thereafter came to light? Would a reviewing court impose liability in such circumstances? Should it?

As the Leavitt case illustrates, often lost in the debate of redemption versus recidivism is another, perhaps greater risk to society if there is to be no opportunity for a college education and a truly fresh start in life. Indeed, even the attorney representing the victim of Parker's sexual assault has stressed that if Parker "doesn't go to school, he ends up on the streets of Harlem. Is that right . . . for society?" (*Providence Journal-Bulletin*, Apr. 22, 1995, p. A1). Should Parker's and Grant's past crimes "condemn [each] to some type of future on the margins of society . . . blind[ed] to the likelihood that college and a good job would probably keep them away from a life of crime whereas the other course makes future criminal activity probable" (*Tampa Tribune*, July 2, 1995, p. 26).

Yet others say more immediate concerns must govern. A mother of a Tufts freshman confesses that she finds Grant's presence at her daughter's school "a little frightening" (*Boston Globe*, Aug. 31, 1995, p. 26), while one GW junior has explained that "I don't care how much you talk about redemption . . . we're the ones who have to deal with [Parker]. He's not going to rape a faculty member. He's going to rape a student" (*Washington Post*, July 16, 1995, p. F1). Whose rights and concerns should prevail in such a case? Are the fears of recidivism an exaggerated reaction to the unknown, or a recognition of a legitimate risk which should be considered in the admission and enrollment process? Should our public policy choices resolve that choice in favor of redemption?

Finally, does the applicable standard of care to be employed in the admissions process differ in those situations where the applicant fails to disclose prior violent or criminal acts, through omission or active misrepresentation? Consider Gina Grant's application and interview with Harvard, as well as the recent cases of James Arthur Hogue, Lon Grammer, and Mauro Cortez, Jr., each of which amply demonstrates the relative ease with which an applicant's past may be concealed during the admissions process. Hogue, a thirty-one-year-old ex-convict from Utah, recreated himself in his application to Princeton University as Alexi Indris-Santana, a "self-schooled" track star from Montana, who had lived in the Mojave desert as a cattle herder, whose artist father had died in a car accident, and whose sculptor mother was dying of leukemia in Switzerland. Princeton admitted Hogue, who thereafter made the Dean's List, the track team, and was offered a spot in the prestigious Ivy Club. Hogue's ruse came to an end only because he was tracked down by Salt Lake City officials for parole violations (*Washington Post*, Aug. 27, 1995, p. C1).

Similarly, Grammer, a former sub-par student at a California community college, gained admission to Yale University by fabricating a straight-A transcript, stellar recommendations, and life as a minor league baseball player, and was not caught until a mere six weeks prior to his scheduled graduation. Likewise, Cortez, a thirty-seven-year-old of Mexican descent, gained admission to Duke University by passing himself off as Maurice de Rothschild, a French heir to a considerable fortune. Asked how Cortez, who spoke no French, was able to fool the university and gain both admission and general acceptance, Duke's assistant dean of admission conceded that the school was "impressed to know what it would be like to be or to know a Rothschild" (*Washington Post*, Aug. 27, 1995, p. C1, quoting *Rolling Stone* Magazine).

Those who believe in redemption, while not condoning the acts of Hogue, Grammer, and Cortez, might point to the fact that each man apparently was a successful student after gaining admission (albeit through misrepresentation), and none among them appears to have participated in any criminal activity or caused injury to fellow students once enrolled. Of course, those concerned about the risk of recidivism might argue with equal fervor that ex-convict Hogue's fraud to gain admission proves that redemption is indeed a risk rarely worth taking, especially when qualified applicants without such baggage stand waiting.

Should the university be held accountable for accepting a misrepresentation and admitting one whose true past they do not know, who then intentionally injures another student? Given our increasingly violent world, should the university be required to conduct some sort of background check to at least verify an applicant's identity and those facts disclosed in his or her application materials, similar to the analogous duty imposed upon employers under the negligent hiring doctrine, discussed above. Is it practical, or advisable, to require college admissions officers to make telephone calls to personal references, high school registrars, and previous employers in order to verify information offered by potential applicants? Privacy concerns, in most instances, could be handled through an appropriate release included on the application form. Yet laying aside increased costs, staffing, and privacy concerns, would such a practice undermine the trust and honor system many universities value as part of their mission and educational message to their communities, by questioning each applicant's commitment to those same values during his or her first exposure to that community? Yet, if a convicted rapist or murderer were to gain admission through a deceit which would have been easily discovered through a limited reference check, and then rape or kill again, how willing would the public and the courts be to forgive the admissions officer who made that decision?

The answer likely rests somewhere in the middle. A university with considerable financial resources or staffing might be held to a higher standard of "reasonable inquiry" than, say, a small college with a limited budget and a one-person admissions office. Another relevant consideration might be the number, ease of use, availability, and knowledge of those methods that would have uncovered the deceit if utilized by the admissions officer.

Recognition of a cause of action for "negligent admitting" would carry certain risks, not the least of which might be increased litigation. Yet perhaps of greater concern would be the potential chilling effect the claim might have on those admissions officers otherwise willing to favor a policy of redemption, yet fearful of university liability (and loss of employment) if that otherwise justifiable faith proves misplaced in a given situation.

Ultimately, we must recognize that there is no way to ascertain with any degree of certainty who is and is not a potential threat to their fellow students. For every Gina Grant or Richie Parker whose past is merely an online search away from being revealed, there may be hundreds of those, like Harvard's

Sinedu Tadesse, for whom no background check or additional inquiry would have revealed the risk of any then-undeveloped future acts of violence. Indeed, as one commentator has noted, "it appears that the only way . . . any university can prevent something like that from happening . . . is to stop admitting students" (*Herald-Sun* [Durham, NC], June 4, 1995, p. G7). Until that time, admissions officers will have to continue to strike an often precarious balance between redemption and recidivism, hoping that their instincts, their experience, the public, and the facts ultimately reward rather than betray them.

Note

1. The authors wish to make clear that these hypotheticals are offered for purposes of illustration and analysis only, and are not intended to imply any opinion as to any predisposition to such conduct on the part of Gina Grant or Richie Parker.

Legal References

Barefoot v. Estelle, 463 U.S. 880 (1983).
Carlsen v. Wackenhut Corp. 868 P.2d 882 (Wash. Ct. App. 1994).
Delaney v. University of Houston, 835 S.W.2d 56 (Tex. 1992).
Eiseman v. State of New York, 511 N.E.2d 1128 (N.Y. Ct. App. 1987).
Garcia v. Duffy, 492 So.2d 435 (Fla. Ct. App. 1986).
Leonardi v. Bradley University, 625 N.E.2d 431 (Ill. Ct. App. 1993).
Mullins v. Pine Manor College, 449 N.E.2d 331 (Ma. 1983).
Nero v. Kansas State University, 861 P.2d 768 (Kan. 1993).
Peterson v. San Francisco Community College, 685 P.2 1193 (Cal. 1984).
Plains Resources, Inc. v. Gable, 682 P.2d 653 (Kan. 1984).
Tanja H. v. Regents of the University of California, 278 Cal. Rptr. 918 (Cal. Ct. App. 1991).

JEROME W. D. STOKES is senior assistant dean of the University of Virginia School of Law in Charlottesville, Virginia.

ALLEN W. GROVES is a partner in the litigation section of the law firm of Glass, McCullough, Sherrill & Harrold in Atlanta, Georgia.

Police training, copyright infringement, and employee crime call for special attention.

A Crime Prevention Wrap-Up: Concluding Comments on Specific Crime Issues

Richard Fossey, Michael Clay Smith

Earlier chapters have moved from the general to the specific in their discussions of campus crime issues. Chapters One through Three were general in nature: Chapter One provided guidance on a crime prevention program; Chapter Two outlined the potential for civil liability in the aftermath of a campus crime; and Chapter Three discussed federal laws and regulations that relate to crime on campus. The next three chapters addressed more specific issues: campus rape in Chapter Four, fraud in Chapter Five, and, in Chapter Six, issues associated with enrolling students who have a criminal history.

This chapter is still more specific, addressing several discrete subjects: campus police training, the application of copyright laws, and special considerations when a college employee is accused of a crime.

Campus Police Training

In the present environment, campus police must be efficient professionals. Gone are the days—or at least they should be—of campus security officers who are just "door rattler" night guards and parking ticket writers. At most colleges and universities today, campus police should be well-trained, well-equipped, and well-supervised. They should be police academy graduates, and hold full legal status as sworn law enforcement officers.

One basic distinction remains, however, between municipal police and their campus counterparts, and that is their ability to be proactive. Because of the overwhelming demands upon them and the limited resources in local government, municipal officers have little time to engage in crime prevention efforts. Instead, municipal police must fill their time reacting to crimes, maintaining order, and responding to calls for assistance. Campus police forces, on the other hand, are in a better position to be proactive. On college campuses, the service area is limited, and institutions have many means of communication with and control over their students and employees. In this environment, campus police have opportunities to engage in serious and broad crime prevention efforts (see Chapter One of this volume).

Specialized training is appropriate for campus police officers. In addition to all the skills of municipal policing, campus officers should have special talents in the areas of interpersonal relations, especially techniques for using interpersonal skills to avoid hostile and violent behavior. They should also be familiar with search and seizure issues relating to dormitories, since this is where most campus police searches take place. In addition, campus police forces should thoroughly understand policies concerning the exercise of lethal force in campus environments. In particular, they should know that the use of firearms and participation in high-speed chases by police vehicles is more restricted in campus settings than in the world at large. Campus police officers should have special training in the investigation of rape and the preservation of evidence in rape cases. Finally, every college or university police officer should know the limits on jurisdiction of campus police.

Mid- and upper-level police managers (sergeants, lieutenants, captains, chiefs) should be trained in the design of campus crime prevention programs. They should know their department's obligations under state and federal privacy and crime reporting laws, and they should be able to interface with other campus constituencies (especially the student affairs and housing functions). In addition, of course, police managers should be trained in leadership skills as well as the nuts and bolts of personnel management.

Copyright Laws and Professors' Course Materials: Unclear Legal Guidance

Although most campus officials are generally aware of federal copyright laws and the way they apply to scholarly writings, some may not realize that these laws may affect the way professors prepare course materials for their classes as well as the operating procedures of campus bookstores and photocopy shops. As we will see, the copyright laws have civil penalties and criminal sanctions that may apply in higher education settings, depending on how copyright materials are reproduced and distributed on college campuses.

Federal copyright laws protect intellectual property from unauthorized reproduction and distribution. The purpose of these statutes is to encourage and reward individual creativity. All original works that have been expressed in a tangible way are protected by the copyright laws, including books, articles, films, photographs, and television and radio broadcasts. A copyright owner has the exclusive right to reproduce and distribute copyrighted work. Moreover, an author need not formally register the original work to obtain the law's protection. The work is protected the moment it is produced in some tangible form.

Copyright owners who believe their copyrights have been violated can bring civil suits for damages against the offenders, and criminal sanctions may be available as well. In most cases, criminal prosecutions occur when the copyright infringement involves fraudulent schemes to copy and produce original works for profit. Under the 1976 copyright act, a general copyright infringement or fraud can be a misdemeanor offense, while record and tape piracy is punishable as a felony (Smith and Fossey, 1995).

At one time it was thought that state colleges and universities could not be penalized for violating the copyright laws other than being enjoined by court order from continuing an unlawful practice. However, the Copyright Remedy Clarification Act of 1990 makes clear that this view is no longer correct. Under the 1990 law, colleges and universities that use their own copying facilities for unauthorized copying can be subjected to damages as if they were a private business (Burgoyne, 1992).

Copyright laws do not prohibit every act of unauthorized copying, however. Materials can be copied under the so-called "fair use" exception, if the copying is done for some educational purpose or as part of a news report or other press activity. To claim the fair use exception, however, the copier must be acting in good faith.

Although the fair use exception cannot be defined with precision, in general it applies when the following conditions are met. Small portions of copyrighted work are copied for classroom work, no charge is made for the copies, the economic loss to the copyright holder is not significant, the material was not originally prepared for educational purposes, and there is no intent to distribute the material to the public.

The application of the copyright laws and the fair use exception to professors' course materials is not clear. In a 1991 lawsuit, *Basic Books, Inc.* v. *Kinko's Graphic Corporation,* a federal court interpreted the law in a case brought by several publishing companies against Kinko's, a private photocopying company. The publishers accused Kinko's of violating the copyright laws by reproducing parts of books as anthologies for college professors who used them as reading packets for various college courses. According to the court opinion, Kinko's had copied portions of twelve of the plaintiffs' copyrighted books, including portions of six books used by a professor in a course that had only three students.

The federal judge ruled against Kinko's, finding that the compilation of anthologies was a copyright violation. In the court's view, the fair use doctrine did not apply. The court's ruling was based on the fact that Kinko's had engaged in a substantial amount of copying and had done so for a profit. The court also believed that the copying activities had hurt the publishing companies' book sales.

In addition, the court determined that Kinko's had not complied with certain classroom guidelines for educational copying, guidelines that appear as part of the legislative history of the 1976 copyright act. Although the guidelines are not part of the law itself, the court looked to the guidelines for an indication of what Congress intended with regard to copying for educational purposes.

Specifically, the court ruled that Kinko's, a for-profit company, could not qualify as an educational copier under the classroom guidelines. Moreover, the court continued, even if it could qualify as an educational copier, it had not complied with the guidelines. Specifically, Kinko's had failed to place a notice of copyright on the copied materials as the guidelines required. In addition, the guidelines were intended to protect "spontaneous" decisions to use copyrighted material for teaching purposes, in circumstances where it would be impractical to ask the copyright owner for permission to copy. In the court's view, Kinko's activities were not spontaneous, since the anthologies were compiled at the beginning of a semester, based on a list of course materials provided by individual professors.

Kinko's was followed by another case, which also signaled judicial intolerance for unauthorized copying of scholarly materials. In *American Geophysical Union* v. *Texaco, Inc.* (1995), a federal appeals court ruled that Texaco's institutional researchers violated the copyright laws when they constructed files made up of photocopied articles from research journals. This practice, the court said, did not constitute fair use of copyrighted material.

Parties in the case had stipulated that the activities of one researcher would be presented as typical of Texaco researchers' copying practices. This researcher's files included eight articles that had been photocopied from one scholarly journal, the *Journal of Catalysis*. Texaco maintained three subscriptions to this journal at the research facility where the designated researcher worked. The fact that the researcher had apparently obtained copies of the articles from journal issues that Texaco had purchased did not prevent the court from finding that a copyright violation had occurred.

In the *Texaco* case, the court made clear that the dispute involved photocopying by institutional scientists, not by individuals pursuing independent research. Thus, the case has no direct application to college professors who copy scholarly articles in pursuit of their own research. Nevertheless, the case is in harmony with the *Kinko's* decision in the sense that the copyrights of scholarly journals prevailed over the interests of scholars.

Kinko's (and to a lesser extent the *Texaco* decision) had a substantial impact on college and university copying operations. After the *Kinko's* decision, many campus copy shops began obtaining written copyright permission before copying material for a professor's course anthology.

A 1996 case, however, contradicts the *Kinko's* decision. In *Princeton University Press* v. *Michigan Document Services, Inc.*, a panel of federal appellate judges upheld a private copy shop's right to reproduce original copyrighted works for the purposes of compiling reading packets for college courses.

In *Princeton University Press,* three publishing companies sued a Michigan copy shop for photocopying portions of the publishers' copyrighted works and packaging them as "coursepacks" for individual college courses. These coursepacks were compiled from a list of materials submitted by University of Michigan college professors, much like the anthologies in the *Kinko's* case. The coursepacks were made up of copyrighted and noncopyrighted material, including journal articles, book excerpts, newspaper articles, test questions, and course syllabi. Without obtaining permission from copyright owners or paying a royalty fee, the copy shop sold the coursepacks for a profit to students who enrolled in the professors' courses. This practice, the publishers maintained, was a clear violation of federal law.

At the trial court level, the case focused on excerpts from six copyrighted books, although a copy shop representative admitted that these works were among several thousand excerpts that the copy shop had copied without obtaining permission. The trial court ruled that the copying was a willful violation of the copyright laws and awarded the publishers $30,000 in damages, $5,000 for each infringement.

A panel of the Sixth Circuit Court of Appeals, however, took a different view, one that was substantially more sympathetic to interests of college professors than the one exhibited in the *Kinko's* decision. Contrary to the *Kinko's* court, the Sixth Circuit panel declined to consult the classroom guidelines to decide the case. Had Congress intended for the guidelines to be the law, the court reasoned, it would have included them in the copyright legislation. Since Congress had not done so, the Sixth Circuit court stated it would look only to the copyright statutes and court cases that had interpreted them to decide the case.

The court began by pointing out that federal copyright law contained a "fair use" exception, permitting a party, in certain limited circumstances, to reproduce copyright materials without the consent of the copyright holder. In order to determine whether a particular use of copyrighted material is fair use, the law requires four factors to be considered: (1) the purpose and character of the use, including whether the copying was done for commercial purposes or for nonprofit educational reasons; (2) the nature of the copyrighted work; (3) the amount of the portion used compared to the copyrighted work as a whole; and (4) the effect of the use on the potential market for or value of the copyrighted work.

All four factors, the court added, must be considered in light of the purpose of the copyright laws, which was not to provide financial rewards for authors, but "to promote the Progress of Science and the useful Arts" (p. 1519). Thus, the court added, when applying the fair use exception to a particular case, courts should balance the reasonable interests of artists and authors in controlling the use of their ideas and society's competing interest in promoting the free flow of ideas and information.

According to the court, an analysis of the first factor—the use to which the copied material is being put—required the court to determine two issues: the extent to which the use of a copyrighted work transforms the original, and the profit or nonprofit motive for the use. A finding of fair use is more likely when no profit is gained and when the use transforms the original by adding something new to the work or altering its character. Fair use is less likely when the use is a mere copy of the original and when the copying is done for profit.

The court acknowledged that the copy shop had copied portions of the plaintiffs' books without altering the text. Nevertheless, the copied portions were used to produce a coursepack, which was a new product. Professors designed coursepacks to further their particular teaching goals. These coursepacks were particularly useful, the court noted, in "newly conceived interdisciplinary courses," because they allowed the professor to gather materials from several established disciplines. Therefore, the court concluded, the coursepacks had at least some slight transformative value.

As for the motive of the use, whether commercial or noncommercial, the court looked beyond the motivation of the copy shop in producing the coursepacks to that of the professors who designed the coursepacks and the students who used them. These professors and their students could reproduce portions of the books individually and assemble the copied materials themselves, so long as they were doing it for an educational purpose and not for a profit. That being the case, the court decided, the professors and students could delegate this task to a copy shop without violating the fair use exception.

Having disposed of the first factor for determining fair use, the court turned to the second factor—the nature of the copyrighted work. With little discussion, the court concluded that this factor merely confirmed that the publishers' books were entitled to copyright protection. It would be the third and fourth factors that determined whether the use to which these copyrighted books was fair use under the law.

The third factor in the fair use test required the court to determine "the amount and substantiality of the portion used in relation to the copyrighted work as a whole." Here, the court stated, it was required to determine whether the portions used in the coursepacks were so substantial that they superseded the copyrighted books and diminished the demand for the originals.

On this point, the publishers might have thought themselves to be on strong ground, since the copy shop had, in some instances at least, copied a significant portion of the publishers' books. With regard to one book, the copied portion comprised 30 percent of the original; and in the other five instances, copied portions ranged from 5 to 18 percent. However, the court determined that even with regard to an extraction of 30 percent, there was no evidence that the copied portion constituted the "heart" of the book, thus in essence replacing the original. Furthermore, the professors who designed the course packs testified that they would not have assigned the original works if photocopied portions were unavailable. Therefore, there was no evidence that the reproduced copies superseded the originals.

Finally, the court considered the fourth factor of the fair use exception: the effect of the reproduction on the potential market and value of the copyrighted works. Relying on an earlier Supreme Court opinion, the Sixth Circuit court ruled that the burden was on the publishing companies to prove that the coursepacks reduced their book sales or that the copying would cause future harm if it became widespread. Since the publishing companies failed to produce evidence that their book sales had been hurt by the coursepacks or that widespread use of coursepacks would affect their markets, the court concluded that the copyright owners had not been harmed.

Before concluding the *Princeton University Press* opinion, the Sixth Circuit panel gave another reason for ruling in favor of the copy shop: the incentive that coursepack distribution gave for authors to write and create. "We confront here an additional consideration. More than one hundred authors declared on the record that they write for professional and personal reasons such as making a contribution to the discipline, providing an opportunity for colleagues to evaluate and critique the authors' ideas and theories, enhancing the authors' professional reputations, and improving career opportunities. These declarants stated that their primary purpose in writing is not for monetary compensation and that they advocate wide dissemination of excerpts from their works via coursepacks without imposition of permission fees" (p. 1524).

In the court's view, the fact that authors often produced higher education materials for nonmonetary reasons was highly relevant. "Copyright law seeks to encourage the use of works to the greatest extent possible without creating undue disincentives to the creation of new works," the court wrote. "The inclusion of excerpts in coursepacks without the payment of permission fees does not deprive authors and inventors of the rewards that the record indicates authors value, such as recognition" (p. 1524).

A finding for the copy shop, the court conceded, would deprive authors of their fair share of the permission fees that publishing companies routinely assess when portions of the authors' works are reproduced in college coursepacks. Nevertheless, while permission fees might be significant to publishing companies, the portion of the fees that authors would get would likely amount to a "mere pittance." In the court's view, the copy shop's use of copyrighted works provided authors with an incentive to create new works.

Princeton University Press v. *Michigan Document Services, Inc.* is welcome news to college professors who feel the need to provide their students with a wide range of course materials but who would not require their students to purchase the material in the form of original copyrighted works. Nevertheless, it is too early to determine whether the 1996 Sixth Circuit panel's decision will supersede the *Kinko's* case as the prevailing law. The panel's decision in *Princeton University Press* was vacated in the spring of 1996 for reconsideration by the entire Sixth Circuit judiciary. It is possible that the new decision, not yet issued, will adopt the view of the *Kinko's* court and rule that professors' course packets constitute copyright violations.

In the meantime, higher education institutions would be wise to review the practices of their in-house copy centers and bookstores to determine whether they are in possible violation of federal copyright law. In addition, colleges and universities should keep faculty members apprised of the unsettled state of copyright law with regard to professors' reading packets and photocopied anthologies. Depending on which of two judicial views becomes generally accepted, college faculty members and their institutions may be running a legal risk by copying and distributing portions of original works as part of college course anthologies.

Special Concerns When Campus Employees Are Accused of a Crime

Copyright violations by campus employees, as vexing as they may be, are of less concern to college administrators than many other kinds of campus misbehavior. Unfortunately, from time to time, college and university employees have engaged in all kinds of very serious criminal activity—from fraud, theft, and forgery to crimes of violence, such as rape or assault.

Campus decision makers must keep two important principles in mind when dealing with an employee's criminal behavior. First, they must coordinate their own investigation with any investigation conducted by law enforcement authorities. Under no circumstances should college authorities take any action that would compromise or impede an ongoing criminal investigation.

Second, state colleges and universities are constitutionally required to afford due process to employees before disciplining or dismissing them for criminal behavior. In essence, due process requires state institutions to provide employees with some kind of fair procedure before depriving them of their job status. At a minimum, due process obligates an institution to give employees notice of the charges and an opportunity to explain themselves at a hearing before a fair decision maker. The purpose of these procedures, of course, is to prevent arbitrary discharges or dismissals based on incorrect information. According to the Supreme Court, in most instances, the employee is entitled to at least an informal hearing before being deprived of his or her job (*Cleveland Board of Education* v. *Loudermill*, 1985).

Private colleges and universities are not constrained by constitutional obligations, but other laws or internal policies may require them to follow fair dismissal procedures as well. In general, private institutions provide the same kinds of checks against capricious or erroneous firing decisions that apply to public institutions.

Some kinds of misconduct provide a clear basis for discharge in almost every instance. College administrators should be aware, however, that federal disability laws can sometimes complicate what would otherwise be a straightforward dismissal case. These laws prohibit employers, both public and private, from discriminating against employees on the basis of a disability. Alcoholism has been recognized as a disability under federal law. Recovered drug addicts (but not employees who currently use drugs) are also protected against employment discrimination.

In several recent cases, alcoholic employees, fired for various kinds of misbehavior, have sued for reinstatement under federal disability laws. In essence, they argued that their misbehavior was linked to a disability and that their discharge constituted discrimination.

For example, in *Maddox* v. *University of Tennessee,* a 1995 case, an assistant football coach was fired by the University of Tennessee after he was arrested and charged with driving while under the influence of alcohol. He sued the university, arguing that he had been discriminated against on account of his alcoholism.

A federal appellate court was unsympathetic. The court upheld the discharge, pointing out that there is a difference between firing someone for unacceptable behavior and firing someone because of a disability. "To hold otherwise," the court observed, "an employer would be forced to accommodate all behavior of an alcoholic which could in any way be related to the alcoholic's use of intoxicating beverages, behavior that would be intolerable if engaged in by a sober employee . . . or an intoxicated but non-alcoholic employee" (p. 847).

The coach had argued that his arrest did not affect his coaching responsibilities, but the appellate court disagreed. As a member of the coaching staff, the court noted, the coach was a representative of the university who served as a role model to athletes. Therefore, the university was entitled to discharge the coach due to the coach's alleged criminal conduct and the publicity that surrounded it.

Maddox v. *University of Tennessee* is likely to become the prevailing view on cases involving the discipline of alcoholic employees. The Americans with Disabilities Act states that drug or alcohol use is not an excuse for otherwise sanctionable misbehavior. Specifically, the law provides that an employer may hold an employee who engages in the illegal use of drugs or who is an alcoholic to the same qualification standards for employment or job performance and behavior that such [employer] holds other employees, "even if any unsatisfactory performance or behavior is related to the drug use or alcoholism of such employee" [42 U.S.C. § 12114(c)(4)].

Similarly, the Rehabilitation Act of 1973 states that the law is not intended to protect alcoholics, "whose current use of alcohol prevents such individual from performing the job in question or whose employment, by reason of such current alcohol abuse, would constitute a direct threat to property or the safety of others" [29 U.S.C. § 706(8)(C)(v)].

Danger of Participating in a Crime Cover-Up

No volume on campus crime issues would be complete without at least a brief discussion of the legal issues associated with failing to report a crime or obstructing a criminal investigation. Indeed, a major reason Congress passed legislation requiring colleges and universities to report their crime statistics was a general suspicion by lawmakers and the public that campus officials were sweeping crime incidents under the rug to avoid bad publicity. In years past, some college administrators hushed up crime incidents, particularly when the perpetrator was a prominent student athlete or the crime incident had the potential for frightening away potential students. The Student Right-to-Know and Campus Security Act (discussed in Chapter Three) was designed to thwart campus crime coverups, requiring colleges and universities to report specific kinds of crime on an annual basis.

But for an individual campus administrator, there is a far more compelling reason not to hush up a campus crime—the potential for criminal liability. In some states, it is a crime itself not to report a crime; and in all states, it is a criminal offense to thwart or impede a criminal prosecution. Obstructing a criminal investigation is defined as obstruction of justice and can lead to stiff fines or even a prison sentence.

A related offense is perjury, knowingly making a false statement under oath. Likewise, it is illegal to urge someone else to make a false sworn statement, whether or not the persuader attempts to procure the perjury with a bribe. Perjury laws apply to any sworn statement, not just those made in court. Knowingly making a false statement in a notarized document, for example, can trigger a state's perjury law.

Conclusion: College Crime Prevention Involves Everyone

Before concluding this chapter, two final points should be emphasized. First, effective college crime prevention must involve the entire campus community. Although crime prevention is a full-time job for the campus police force and a few key administrators, it is also a general responsibility of student services personnel, the maintenance department, faculty, and students. Everyone in the campus community has an obligation to act prudently to avoid becoming a crime victim and to be watchful for signs of possible criminal activity.

Second, a crime prevention program is not something that can be put into place and forgotten. An effective crime prevention program requires an ongoing crime awareness program for new students and employees. Campus security must be constantly monitored for such problems as inadequate lighting, overgrown shrubbery, or careless dormitory security.

References

Burgoyne, R. A. "The Copyright Remedy Clarification Act of 1990: State Educational Institutions Now Face Significant Monetary Exposure for Copyright Infringement." *Journal of College and University Law*, 1992, *18* (3), 367–389.

Smith, M. C., and Fossey, R. *Crime on Campus: Legal Issues and Campus Administration*. Phoenix, Ariz.: Oryx Press and American Council on Education, 1995.

Legal References

American Geophysical Union v. *Texaco, Inc.*, 60 F.3d 913 (2nd Cir. 1995).

Basic Books, Inc. v. *Kinko's Graphics Corp.*, 758 F. Supp. 1522 (S.D.N.Y. 1991).

Cleveland Board of Education v. *Loudermill*, 470 U.S. 564 (1985).

Maddox v. *University of Tennessee*, 62 F.3d 843 (6th Cir. 1995).

Princeton University Press v. *Michigan Document Services, Inc.*, 74 F.3d 1512 (6th Cir. 1996), vacated, 74 F.2d. 1528.

RICHARD FOSSEY is associate professor of education law and policy at Louisiana State University.

MICHAEL CLAY SMITH is professor of criminal justice at the University of Southern Mississippi.

INDEX

ORDERING INFORMATION

NEW DIRECTIONS FOR HIGHER EDUCATION is a series of paperback books that provides timely information and authoritative advice about major issues and administrative problems confronting every institution. Books in the series are published quarterly in Spring, Summer, Fall, and Winter and are available for purchase by subscription and individually.

SUBSCRIPTIONS cost $52.00 for individuals (a savings of 35 percent over single-copy prices) and $79.00 for institutions, agencies, and libraries. Standing orders are accepted. New York residents, add local tax for subscriptions. (For subscriptions outside the United States, add $7.00 for shipping via surface mail or $25.00 for air mail. Orders *must be prepaid* in U.S. dollars by check drawn on a U.S. bank or charged to VISA, MasterCard, or American Express.)

SINGLE COPIES cost $20.00 plus shipping (see below) when payment accompanies order. California, New Jersey, New York, and Washington, D.C., residents, please include appropriate sales tax. Canadian residents, add GST and any local taxes. Billed orders will be charged shipping and handling. No billed shipments to post office boxes. (Orders from outside the United States *must be prepaid* in U.S. dollars by check drawn on a U.S. bank or charged to VISA, MasterCard, or American Express.)

SHIPPING (SINGLE COPIES ONLY): one issue, add $5.00; two issues, add $6.00; three issues, add $7.00; four to five issues, add $8.00; six to seven issues, add $9.00; eight or more issues, add $12.00.

ALL PRICES are subject to change.

DISCOUNTS FOR QUANTITY ORDERS are available. Please write to the address below for information.

ALL ORDERS must include either the name of an individual or an official purchase order number. Please submit your order as follows:
  Subscriptions: specify series and year subscription is to begin
  Single copies: include individual title code (such as HE82)

MAIL ALL ORDERS TO:
  Jossey-Bass Publishers
  350 Sansome Street
  San Francisco, California 94104-1342

FOR SUBSCRIPTION SALES OUTSIDE OF THE UNITED STATES, contact any international subscription agency or Jossey-Bass directly.

OTHER TITLES AVAILABLE IN THE
NEW DIRECTIONS FOR HIGHER EDUCATION SERIES
Martin Kramer, Editor-in-Chief